Conflicts in the Northeast
Internal and External Effects

Conflicts in the Northeast
Internal and External Effects

Editors

Sanjoy Hazarika
&
V R Raghavan

Published for
Centre for Security Analysis
Chennai, India

Vij Books India Pvt Ltd
New Delhi, India

Published   by

Vij Books India Pvt Ltd

2/19, Ansari Road, Darya Ganj
New Delhi - 110002
Phones: 91-11- 43596460, 91-11-47340674
Fax: 91-11-47340674
e-mail : vijbooks@rediffmail.com
web : www.vijbooks.com

Centre for Security Analysis
"9-B" Ninth Floor,
Chesney Nilgiri, 71, Ethiraj Salai,
Egmore, Chennai-600008
Tamil Nadu, India
+91-44-65291889
office@csa-chennai.org
www.csa-chennai.org

The views and opinions presented in this book are of the author(s) of the chapters in the book and not necessarily that of the Centre for Security Analysis, Chennai, India.

First Published : 2011

ISBN 13 : 978-93-81411-12-4

Acknowledgement

The Centre for Security Analysis (CSA) has undertaken a three year research project **Internal Conflicts and Transnational Consequences** supported by the John. D and Catherine. T MacArthur Foundation. This volume is part of the ongoing project and its publication has been possible by the project grant.

TABLE OF CONTENTS

Appendix

`

FOREWORD

Northeast India comprising of seven states of Assam, Arunachal Pradesh, Manipur, Meghalaya, Mizoram, Nagaland and Tripura have endured the onslaught of ethnic-based armed conflicts for the last half a century or more. It makes India's Northeast region one of South Asia's most disturbed areas.

The instability in Northeast India is characterized by two distinct factors –ethnic clashes among the indigenous groups and political movement against the Union Government. The conflicting dynamics in the Northeast ranges from insurgency for secession to insurgency for autonomy, from terrorism to ethnic clashes, to problems of continuous inflow of migrants and the fight over resources. Moreover, vested interests and inter tribal and inter factional rivalry have led militant groups to continually clash among themselves, plunging the region in a vicious cycle of militancy, social violence and lack of economic growth. These armed conflicts have given impetus to small arms proliferation, narcotics trade and a parallel economy.

Northeast India's porous border with China, Nepal, Bangladesh and Myanmar adds trans-border ramifications to the conflict. The trans-border nature of the ethnic and religious affinities provides a fertile ground for external involvement. As a result, militant groups operating in Northeast receive political as well as financial support from across the border. The porous nature of the border makes it easier for militants to operate and maintain military and logistical bases in the neighbouring countries.

Over the years, both the state and the central government have used various tactics from negotiations to military operations to bring stability and to curtail militancy in the region. Central political leadership has always shown a willingness to meet legitimate grievances of the people of the Northeastern region. The Government introduced the institution of Autonomous District Councils (ADC) to give the region's tribal groups a limited self-rule by providing them greater control over local resources and protection of cultural identity. Where a particular group was not satisfied with this limited accommodation, as was the case with the Nagas, the government went ahead and created separate provinces for them, providing local leaders with more effective control over resources and power. Each of these interventions has had associated political and economic costs. Besides developmental and economic costs, other sectors have also been affected *viz*, law and order, education, health and governance.

The Central Government of late has shown willingness to negotiate with many insurgent groups like, NSCN-(IM), NSCN (K), NDFB, some factions of ULFA and has arranged for cease fire too. Some more groups are in the process to negotiating ceasefire agreements with the Government. Nevertheless, the region remains a potential tinderbox. Political order and security in Northeast India, both for the state and its citizens, nevertheless remains elusive. Prolonged violence in the region has also impacted on the character of the state and on its democratic credentials. The urgency to restore peace is therefore strong.

As a part of its ongoing project on Internal *Conflicts and Transnational Consequences*, the Centre for Security Analysis (CSA) organized a study to understand the consequences of the armed conflicts in Northeast India in association with Centre for North- East Studies and Policy Research (C-NES). These studies were presented at a seminar organized in New Delhi in July 2010. The former Union Home Secretary Mr. G K Pillai who was a special invitee had an informal discussion with the paper presenters and other invitees. He appreciated and encouraged the role of NGOs in taking such initiatives to study problems of the Northeast and hoped that such efforts would help in generating better understanding of each others' views besides developing mutual respect and trust.

CSA in its effort to bring out a new approach to study the internal conflicts and consequences has drawn researchers from varied backgrounds who had the experience of working on these conflicts as a part of the policy making or academic community. This volume provides a wide-ranging and significant insight into the internal and external consequences of the armed conflicts in the Northeastern region of India.

V R Raghavan
Lt Gen (Retd)
President
Centre for Security Analysis

INTRODUCTION

Sanjoy Hazarika

For nearly two decades, the Government of India has waxed eloquent about its "Look East Policy"; from the time of Mr PV Narasimha Rao to Dr. Manmohan Singh, this concept (if not the "policy" itself, if it can be called as such –for it has been high on rhetoric but low on focus, objectives, muscle and delivery) has drawn much interest and criticism in the region of Northeastern India (NER).

Although the discussions and papers for the two-day seminar organized by the Centre for Security Analysis (CSA) and the Centre for North East Studies and Policy Research (C-NES) which have resulted in this book were not focused around the Look East Policy (LEP), almost every paper reflected on the concerns and issues that the states of the region have not just with New Delhi but with their immediate and distant neighbours: Myanmar, Bhutan, Bangladesh, even Tibet and parts of South East Asia to where many ethnic groups trace their ancestry and route of migration. The challenges before the region and India are driven by internal pressures of conflict, pressure on natural resources and perceptions of "the other"; in turn, these have produced a range of varying impacts in the neighbourhood, including security linkages between Governments, between armed non-State groups and the State as well as among themselves (often, encouraged by governments), migration as well as how policies which have repercussions on neighbouring nations are often driven by internal objectives of the national governments or policy makers.

Indeed, many of these conflicts, it could be argued, are often preceded by the clash of ideas, not just the immediacy of a problem of an "insurgency" or an "agitation." In addition, the location of the region, politically but also

1

geographically, has a fundamental bearing on it and its people who aspire for different goals and how they try to reach these goals. The NER has borders with four countries: Myanmar, Bhutan, Bangladesh and Tibet/China and, as is well known, connected to the Indian mainland by a narrow stretch of land popularly called the Chicken's Neck.

The papers (as well as Niketu Iralu's keynote remarks) look at different aspects of the region. These include an overview on the Economic Impacts of Conflicts by Prof. Mohendro Singh. After reviewing the various stages of conflict, he remarks that a virtuous growth cycle is difficult in the Northeast because of a range of factors. He identifies them as "burden of history, hurdle of politics, presence of many ethnic groups, hill terrains and weak governance." Geography, he adds, has "conspired with economics, faulty planning and poor implementation to give the region a weak hand," beginning with the 1947 Partition which established a physical distance between markets, hinterlands and traditional neighbours (e.g. Syhlet and Mymensingh with today's Meghalaya state). Prof. Mohendra reflects on the impacts of "unrest" on the economy of the region with a close look at his home state of Manipur.

Dr. Samir Kumar Das describes his essay as "an attempt to understand (the) ULFA phenomenon - neither in complete isolation from its externalities including the known framework of Indo-Bangladesh relations nor completely within that framework - but *beyond* either of them." He zeroes in on the fundamental issues that have evolved with regard to the United Liberation Front of Asom (ULFA) and its armed struggle against India. He asserts that "the ULFA phenomenon cannot simply be reduced to the high and low of Indo-Bangladesh relations as much as the latter cannot simply be reduced to the ULFA phenomenon." Dr. Das says that his paper "seeks to tell a story of those forces and processes which are not mediated by any bilateral or for that matter international relations and therefore remain relatively outside the control of any nation-state, and most importantly, how they affect and impinge on both ULFA and the course of Indo-Bangladesh relations. It also makes a call for accordingly reorienting and calibrating India's external policy towards the militants and insurgents of the Northeast."

By the time the workshop was completed and the papers assigned and edited, the political situation in Assam and to a substantial degree in other parts of the North East had changed considerably, with the major faction in ULFA under its Chairman Arabinda Rajkhowa eschewing arms, accepting a Constitutional arrangement and preparing for peace talks where a negotiated settlement could be thrashed out. A strong but small element under the breakaway army chief Paresh Baruah says it refuses to accept this process but it is in a minority. Indeed, public fatigue with conflict and lack of economic growth is turning into resentment and anger against those seeking to block peace building.

Dr. Das emphasizes the research methodological "mess" which, he feels, characterizes the quality of published work on the North-eastern region without adding substantially to the scholarship of issues located there. He also feels that the pro-Islamic anti-India hold on Bangladesh was so strong at one time that Sheikh Hasina could do little to throw the Bangladesh-based ULFA and other rebel groups out of her country during her first term of office. Things changed after she returned with a thumping majority and proceeded to just do that from 2009 December onward.

That was a skilful demonstration of the security-diplomatic nexus that drives policies between neighbours and which change as the dynamics of internal political situations change. In this case, an anti-India government led by Khaleda Zia was replaced by Ms. Sheikh Hasina who was friendlier, at the very least, towards India. Tracing a three-stage dimension to ULFA's connections with Dhaka, Dr. Das warns against the oversimplification of a complex relationship between neighbours (and even suggests significantly that despite present assertions of bonhomie that "ULFA's ties with Bangladesh are likely to survive the Bangladeshi State's recent crackdown on ULFA leaders and cadres." The paper competently looks at ULFA's changing postures on the core issue of illegal migration from Bangladesh which has often torn Assam apart and the future of the peace negotiations.

At the core of India-Bangladesh relations lies the factor of migration from our neighbour into this country's eastern sector, a flow that now encompasses many towns, cities and rural districts of India, stretching as

3

far as Rajasthan and Maharashtra and down South past the Vindhyas. This phenomenon of migration is essentially, in my view, a flow of labour from a country; it is spurred by a belief that many can eke out a better living in India. This has been borne out by field research that have been conducted in both countries[1], by other scholars such as Prof. Rehman Sobhan of the Centre for Policy Dialogue in Dhaka, Prof. Mahendra Lama of Sikkim University, as well as official government studies and reports in the popular media.

In "Migration Mantra and the Bangladesh Northeast Conundrum," Dr. Sanjib Kakoty briefly examines some of these issues and provides a background to the concerns that continue to trouble Assam and other North-eastern states even today. He mentions also another issue that has caught the imagination of the world in recent years – the phenomenon of a rise in the level of oceanic waters fuelled by global warning. He speaks of "the very real probability of a large part of Bangladesh getting inundated, due to rising sea levels to be brought about by global warming. Where would the millions go? Obviously these ecological migrants would be forced to the other parts of the world, which would particularly include India and Assam. Are we prepared for this possible deluge?" Obviously, there are no easy answers to such questions and challenges although they must spur the international community – and neighbours – to cooperate and support each other, through financial, ecological (including life style changes by using less energy) and social measures.

In her paper, Vijayalakhsmi Brara discusses the interesting concept of the "opening of the Eastern Door" and tries to weave into the discussion the role of India's much-vaunted Look East Policy. That "after seven generations" of agreeing under an earlier King to open up to the West i.e. other parts of India, had the time come to be more open to other eastern influences. "But, then again, why this recent upsurge and a wave towards the revival of the phrase *Nongpok Thong Hangba?* Why does Manipur again want to look towards the east," despite the violence she suffered at the hands of Burmese rulers in the early part of the 19th century? Dr.

---

[1] Sanjoy Hazarika,   (New Delhi:Penguin Books India Ltd, 2000)

4

Brara explores with some angst the easy familiarity with which travelers from her state find themselves in South-east Asia and the often brutal discrimination bordering on racial stereotyping that Northeastern students face in places like Delhi. Such experiences make the "opening of the eastern door" more appealing. Indeed, the way young Manipuris have embraced Korean cultural icons, music, movies and stars is an interesting phenomenon which she comments upon, partly as a reaction to the "mainstreaming" project of the conservative right-wing as well as the visible "Indianization" all around them. It also is a reaction to the conduct that encapsulates the daily prejudice which they face in other parts of the country.

In his detailed overview of the Naga situation, so critical to the understanding of the issues that affect the NER and its neighbourhood, Prof Udayon Misra paints a masterly canvas of the range of the problem, plumbing its depth as well as the vision of its leaders as well as their internal squabbling which devastated the movement and the lives of ordinary people. He minces no words about India's blunders with its violations of human rights and regrouping of villages but also describes, step by step, the growth of the different factions and their struggle for supremacy and relations with the Indian State. Prof. Misra writes: "Till recently, however, the two most important issues posed by the Naga movement have been (a) the question of Naga sovereignty/self-determination and (b) the question of an unified Nagalim/Greater Nagalim. To this has now been added the question of reconciliation among the different segments of the Naga movement." While the issue of a unified Nagalim is bound to face insurmountable hurdles in the form of opposition from the neighbouring states and would also involve the changing of existing state boundaries under the provisions of Articles 2-3 of the Constitution of India, it is also bound to create problems for the Naga populations residing in these states. The blockade of Manipur showed, among other things, that the sympathies of the peoples of the neighbouring states lay largely with the people of Manipur and this, in turn, is bound to affect New Delhi's perception of the problem, all its dilly-dallying notwithstanding. What is further important is that the insistence on a unified Nagalim is bound to eat into the common struggle and solidarity of the people's of the northeastern region for a truly federal relationship with the Indian Union.

A look at Tripura's insurgencies and their links with Bangladesh as well as the inner divisions among rival armed groups is an important part of Jayanta Bhattacharya's essay on Tripura, which also recounts the Communist-ruled state's "success story" in combating these uprisings. There is an interesting section here on the spillover of ethnic violence against the jhumia (farmers depending on shifting cultivation) Reangs or Brus in neighbouring Mizoram and their flight to Tripura where they have struggled to survive on pitiful rations in cramped relief camps while their leaders and the Mizoram Government have failed to sort out an acceptable settlement. Despite pressure from New Delhi and visits by Central officials, the flight and plight of the 37,000 internally displaced Reangs in Tripura remained unresolved for over a decade.

This appears time and again to be at the heart of an cyclic, unbreakable and unresolvable issue in the whole region, and one that strikes a common resonance, providing a common platform — the role and impact of "insiders" and "outsiders" in culturally sensitive spaces and the timeframe in which they are defined as one or the other, whether it is the "illegal migrants" of Assam, the Reangs of Mizoram and the Chakmas and Hajongs of Arunachal Pradesh. There are the Pnars of Karbi Anglong who have fled Assam for the safety of their "home" state of Meghalaya —this in turn raises another question, both for larger or small communities: is the sense of a "safe" homeland so attractive as to make a community or an individual forsake their roots in the place where they had earlier settled?

Some of the papers challenge a set of assumed Impunities: the Impunity of the State, the Impunity of non-state (armed) actors; Impunity as a tool to coerce groups into submission, to drive the so-called development process without – naturally given the nature of Impunity — either the consent or the basic right of consultation or dissent that is inherent in a democratic process. The nature of Impunity is a reflection of the nature and character of the State –there is little concern about the impacts of what it does or seeks to do: it is not just conducting an "operation" but actions whose impacts remain embedded in the minds and spirits of people for decades afterward. There is little recompense, virtually no information as to how people can get justice, no effort to reach out and heal.

This remains an issue that also needs to be addressed at length, elsewhere, in a separate volume – although it is partly reflected upon by Prof. Misra in his essay with regard to the processes of reconciliation among the Naga feuding groups. One of the principal democratic deficits that can be pinpointed in India is that in places such as Nagaland, Mizoram and Manipur as well as Assam and Tripura, where some of the sharpest conflicts have taken place and some of the worst "excesses" or atrocities –by security forces and the non-State armed groups –few have come from anywhere in India to listen to the trauma of victims. This is an area where "civil society" in the broadest understanding of that much-misused phrase, needs to do far more if old nightmares and wounds are not to be reopened and new conflicts ignited.

I would like to place my appreciation on record to Lt Gen VR Raghavan, the President, CSA, for his leadership on this issue, to his colleagues, especially Brig K Srinivasan, who have conducted the organization of the conference and support to C –NES with such commitment, and for the extreme patience they have shown in the delays caused by the editing of this book, especially this Introductory Chapter. I am grateful also to Mr GK Pillai, then Union Home Secretary, for coming and speaking to us at a special session which was off –the-record, and to each one of my colleagues who have contributed to this book. I also wish to express my appreciation to Ms Priyamrita Chatterjee, C –NES' office manager, who handled so many issues with diligence and extreme and quiet competence.

IMPACT OF CONFLICTS IN THE NORTHEAST WITH SPECIAL REFERENCE TO MANIPUR

N. Mohendro Singh

The development experience of the world witnesses an uneasy phenomenon of a marked rise in the conflict related deaths along with the higher educational advancement, scientific achievement and technological progress, thereby questioning the very core foundation of knowledge and literacy. It appears that while the world has changed a lot, man has not sufficiently changed in the real sense of the term. In fact, one can expect higher sense of universal values of humanity and sound reason with the growth of education and massive interventions in the human resource development.

16th century records only 1.6 millions of conflict-related-deaths accounting for 0.32 per cent of the world population. 17th century goes much ahead with 6.1 millions of conflict-related-deaths accounting for 1.05 per cent of the world population. 19th century was marked by a sharp increase from 7.0 millions in 18th century to 19.4 millions accounting for 1.65 per cent of the world population. Exceptionally high rate of conflict related deaths is reported in the 20th century. It touched three digits of 109.7 millions accounting for 4.35 per cent of the world population –very disturbing. India and its Northeastern Region also have their "share contribution".

Table – 1: Rising Conflicts and Loss of Human Lives

Period	Conflict deaths (million)	Conflict related death as % to world population
16th Century	1.6	0.32
17th Century	6.1	1.05
18th Century	7.0	0.92
19th Century	19.4	1.65
20th Century	109.7	4.35

Source: - Conflict deaths data: Sivarad 1991, 1996. Twentieth century Population data, U.N. 2005, Human Development Report Office interpolation based on Sykes 2004 – quoted by the Second Administrative Reforms Commission, Feb. 2008 – 7th Report P – 4.

During 2003-2006, in India there were 6267 Naxal violent incidents that took toll of 2436 lives. The incidence of violence is fairly high in the Northeast; a region of "stable anarchy".[1] In this region 7911 incidents took place and 6481 people were killed during 2001-2006.

Table – 2: Naxal Violence, 2003 – 2006

Year	Incidents	Deaths
2003	1597	515
2004	1553	677
2006	1509	678
Total	6267	2436

Source: Annual Report of Ministry of Home Affairs, 2006 – 07

---

[1] Lt. Gen. S.K. Pillai, "Three Matryoshkas: Ethnicity, Autonomy & Governance," paper presented at a seminar on   organized by the Institute for Conflict Management at India International Centre, New Delhi, on June 25-27, 2001

Table – 3: Incidence of Violence in the Northeast

Head	2001	2002	2003	2004	2005	2006
Incidence of violence	1335	1312	1332	1234	1332	1366
Extremists killed	572	571	523	404	405	395
Security personnel killed	175	147	90	110	70	76
Civilians killed	660	454	494	414	393	309

Source: GOI: Annual Report of Ministry of Home Affairs, 2006 – 07

Then, what is conflict which looks so dangerous and annihilating? A conflict is said to be a situation between two or more groups who see their perspectives and standpoints as incompatible. In other words, the deep sense of incompatibility lies at the root of conflict. Conflict is considered bad as it is accompanied by tension, violence and killing. In other words, the mindless acts of violence are let loose. There is another school of thought according to which conflicts are desirable as they can create change. Conflict may also stimulate a new sense of competitiveness and initiate a new directional departure. Conflict may be a destroyer as a source of violence and may also be a creator as a source of development. Of course, it is very difficult to imagine a situation characterized by the complete absence of conflict as a man is a member of various groups and he has multiple identities with reference to geographical origin, gender, caste, class, language, ethnicity, profession and social commitment. The ugly heads of open defiance and violent assertion born out of various forms of conflict has camouflaged the charm of a genuine multi-cultural society with genuine emotional integration. Rather, in India, we are gradually drifted towards a new phenomenon of "fractured pluralism". The tantalizing phenomenon of discontentment raises a number of questions. The basic question is who gets what, when and

11

how? Is time really the best healer? What is the quality of so-called interventions? How far we have taken care of material dimension of conflicts? How long the increasing concentration of power, wealth and status be allowed to continue? What is the way out of the vicious circle of hardened poverty and multiple deprivations? Does it not amount to dehumanization without limit?

Conflict is not a single-event phenomenon but a dynamic process having a life cycle. Unless it is well-managed and taken care of, it leads to a stalemate in the long run. The first stage is of individual and societal tensions created out of a feeling of injustice and victimization; the feeling of being wronged. This is followed by a "Latent Conflict" where the expression of simmering discontentment is found in various forms of requests and demands. This is an opportune time for administration to address the grievances.

In the event of timely warning not being attended to, the disrupting forces gain momentum. The unattended grievances, overlooked concerns and neglected tensions lead to accentuation of the situation. The stand of the aggrieved and opposing groups gets hardened and they take the issue to the streets in the form of demonstrations, processions, bandhs, blockades etc.

Once the seed of escalation has started showing its ugly heads, a small spark may lead to larger eruption of violence. It turns into a major event. The prolonged unsolved problems turn into a crisis. This is the fifth stage of the cycle. Ultimately the eruption takes place at regular intervals at any point of time anywhere. And thus, the state machinery is exposed to a stalemate. In short, there is a need for a built-in mechanism for 1) understanding early warnings, 2) for undertaking timely analysis and 3) for acting on appropriate measures. What do we need now is a strong institutional mechanism to enforce public law and set a new social order. This calls for strict application of eight components of good governance such as 1) broad based participation, 2) rule of law, 3) transparency, 4) accountability, 5) responsiveness, 6) efficiency, 7) equity and 8) vision. The new ground for a **Development Dialogue** with a shared vision could have a potential for breaking the ice. Social scientists make a strong point for a new focus on the **conflict mapping** for a hopeful initiative towards a conflict resolution; as the conflict mapping covers a wide range of stakeholders and concerns namely, *"all parties", all goals", "all issues", "forgotten issues" and "forgotten goals".* It is not merely a question of fire-fighting but a question of confidence-building exercise through a broad-based participation for equitable distribution of benefits and justice.

Northeastern Region

The Northeastern Region represents 8 per cent of the total geographical area of India with only 40 million people (4 per cent of the total population of the country). The region is a visible victim of regional disparity and fundamental backwardness.

> *"Troubled by history and geo-politics, the North East has remained one of the most backward regions of the country. The trauma of partition in 1947 not only took the region backwards by at least a quarter century, but also placed hurdles on future economic progress. It isolated the region, sealed both land and sea routes for commerce and trade, and served access to traditional markets and the gateway to the East and South-East Asia – the Chittagong port in East Bengal (now Bangladesh). It distanced the approach to the rest of India by confining connectivity to a narrow 27-km-wide Siliguri corridor, making it a 'remote land' and constraining access for movement of goods and people. The uneasy relationship with most of the neighbouring countries has not helped the cause of development of the region either with 96 per cent of the boundary of the region forming international borders, private investment has shied away from the region." (North eastern Region Vision 2020).[2]*

---

[2] Ministry of Development of Northeastern Region and North Eastern Council, "Peace, Progress and Prosperity in Northeastern Region: Vision 2020, NER Vision 2020, Vol I, 2008, 2 available online at http://mdoner.gov.in/writereaddata/newsimages/final6963338914.pdf

Now the region is making best possible attempt to come up to the level of national average by 2020. As a part of necessary exercise the Northeastern Region (NER) has to register the annual average growth rate of 10 per cent during 2007-2012, 13.67 per cent during 2012-2017 and 16.37 per cent during 2017-2020 as against the national average of 9 per cent during the said periods.

In the same fashion the growth rate of per capita GSDP should also be made much higher than the national average. While the increase of national average of per capita GSDP is 7.61 per cent per annum during 2007-2020, that of the NER should be 11.64 per cent.

Besides, there is additional economic responsibility for the NER. This region has to play a crucial role in the progressive materialization of the Look East Policy of India. The region, by virtue of its strategic location, should connect India to the dynamic and booming economies of the South East Asian countries.

To reap perceptible benefit and also to forge ahead the competitive participation, the home ground of the region needs to be strengthened to enable it to act as a major source of local manufacture; — not as a transit corridor. The cultural component in the development strategy could be our advantage. B. G. Varghese rightly observes "the region is Indian Mongoloid and culturally part of South East Asia". The Indo-Myanmar Border Trade, 1994-95 was opened through Moreh, (Manipur) keeping this hard reality in view. The region is facing tough time to prepare itself to take advantage of the "Economic Miracle" of the South East Asian economy.

But unfortunately the NER has to work under many odds and constraints imposed by burden of history, hurdle of politics, presence of many ethnic groups, hill terrains and weak governance. Geography has conspired with economics, faulty planning and poor implementation to give the region a weak hand. The region has suffered much for a quite long time. Even before the completion of the required phases of reconstruction of the economy on all basic fronts such as road, power, water, education and health, after the partition of 1947, the region has been exposed to the tantalizing effects of prolonged instability.

Today the region is passing through a new phase of conflict situation of unrest, bandhs, economic blockades and other violent activities sponsored and spearheaded by a number of insurgent and social outfits. Let us look at Manipur "the most insurgency ridden state with 15 violent outfits".

In connection with the undesirable "activities" of the insurgent organizations in Manipur, the Second Administrative Reforms Commission of India, (2008), observes: —

> *"Today militant organizations are virtually running a parallel government in many districts of Manipur and they are able to influence the decision of the State Government in awarding contracts, supply orders and appointments in government services. It is also reported that militant organizations indulge in wide spread extortion and hold 'courts' and dispense justice in their areas of influence. Such a situation results in erosion of faith of the people in the constitutional governance machinery".[3]*

The bandhs and blockades and other violent events are largely manifestations of conflicts. And the internal dislocations and negative externalities ultimately unsettle the age-old socio economic equations. The negative impacts of bandhs and blockades tell heavily upon three sectors.

Economic Sector

In Manipur, during 2004-05, number of days of **bandhs** were 20 and the loss incurred amounted to Rs. 5.34 crore a day. The annual loss was Rs. 106.80 crore. The year 2005-06 became worse with 48 days of bandhs resulting in the loss per day of Rs 6.13 crore and annual loss of Rs. 294.24 crore. The year 2006-07 had more or less the same bitter experience with 42 days of bandhs, incurring daily loss of Rs. 6.88 crore and annual loss of Rs. 288.96 crore.

---

[3] GOI,   ", Second Administrative
    Reforms Committee, Seventh Report ,2008

Much more demoralizing is the event of continued **economic blockade** on National Highways 39 and 53, the two lifelines of Manipur. The **duration** of economic blockade ranges from **2 days to 69 days.** The two longest are **69-day blockade** in **2010** and **52-day blockade in 2005.** With 60 days of economic blockade in 2004-05, Manipur suffered the daily loss of Rs. 2.32 crore and annual loss of Rs. 139.20 crore. The year 2005-06 suffered more with the annual loss of Rs. 258.99 crore. The year 2006-07 was also equally bad with the annual loss of Rs. 231.77 crore as a consequence of 77 days of economic blockade. The longest single economic blockade of 69 days in 2010 (April 12 to June 19) on National Highway–39 (Imphal-Dimapur-Guwahati) was most demoralizing with the complete failure of movement of goods and services. The loss amounted to Rs. 276 crore. The total loss suffered by Manipur economy on account of economic blockades and bandhs was Rs. 246 crore in 2004-05, Rs. 553.23 crore in 2005-06 and Rs. 520.73 crore in 2006-07. The annual loss accounts for nearly 7 per cent of the GSDP. The per capita loss due to bandhs and blockades was Rs. 996 in 2004-05 and in 2005-06 it rose to Rs. 2196, followed by Rs. 2027 in 2006-07 (See Tables, 4, 5 and 6)

Table – 4: Loss suffered by Manipur Economy on account of economic blockade on NH-39 and 53

Year	Nos. of Economic Blockade	Economic Loss per day (Rs. Crore)	Total loss due to blockade (Rs. Crore)
2004-05	60	2.32	139.20
2005-06	97	2.67	258.99
2006-07	77	2.01	231.77
April 12 - June 17, 2010 i.e. 66 days (single blockade)	69	4.00	276

Source: Govt. of Manipur, Directorate of Economics and Statistics

Table – 5: Loss suffered by Manipur Economy on account of bandhs

Year	Nos. of Bandhs	Loss per day (Rs. Crore)	Total loss (Rs. Crore)
2004-05	20	5.34	106.80
2005-06	48	6.13	294.24
2006-07	42	6.88	288.96

Source: Govt. of Manipur, Directorate of Economics and Statistics

Table – 6: Total Loss suffered by Manipur Economy on account of economic blockade and bandhs in Crores

Year	Economic Blockade	Bandhs	Total Loss	Loss per capita (Rs.)
2004-05	139.20	106.80	246.00	996
2005-06	258.99	294.24	553.23	2196
2006-07	231.77	288.9	520.73	2027

Source:-Govt. of Manipur, Directorate of Economics and Statistics

The price hike is not new in Manipur. Normally the price behaviour in the retail market is higher by 20 per cent than the national average. But during the prolonged economic blockades, the prices of essential commodities increase three fold. The price of petrol per litre is Rs. 100 to Rs. 140. The price of kerosene also increases to Rs. 100 per litre. The price of diesel increases to Rs. 80 per litre. The all-time high price of LPG of Rs. 1200 to

1500 per cylinder is really agonizing. The cost escalation touched all time high. The expenditure on essential items multiplied with a heavy onslaught on the meager saving of the people in the state.

Black marketing and adulteration are concomitant phenomenon of the acute scarcity of essential commodities and unprecedented hike in prices. In fact, the people in the state have to go back to the scramble for survival rather than going forward with the strategy for development.

The sectoral loss fluctuates from sector to sector. Since both backward and forward linkages are local-based with a principal aim of producing to meet domestic requirements, the agricultural sector does not suffer much. But the secondary sector which require larger forward and backward linkages suffers economic loss to the extent of 80-85 per cent because of bandhs and to the tune of 36 per cent as a consequence of blockades. Construction suffers 27 per cent loss on account of blockades whereas bandhs affect to the extent of 78.74 per cent. The service sector which accounts for 42 per cent of the state domestic product suffers much during bandhs. In fact, the activities in trade and hospitality are greatly affected during bandhs almost 100 per cent, while during blockades only 84 per cent. The public administration, business and legal services and banking and insurance activities also suffer the loss from 40 per cent in public administration to 69.45 per cent in business and legal services and 100 per cent in banking and insurance activities during bandhs.

The second component of loss on the economic front is the emergence of hostile investment atmosphere. Frequent and unexpected imposition of economic blockade and call of bandhs by the underground and other civil organizations create a hostile investment atmosphere punctuated by:

- Insecurity of life,
- Insecurity of investment,
- Insecurity of business,
- Insecurity of employment and
- Disruption in market connectivity.

The four core areas of sound investment such as stability and security, regulation and taxation, finance and infrastructure and worker and labour market get sudden setback. Link between effort and reward is distorted. Uncertain response becomes a way of life. These pernicious activities raise the fixed capital, delay the productive process and invite a beginning of growthless life.

> *"Nothing so undermines the investment climate as the outbreak of armed conflict. Capital of all kinds— human, physical and social – is destroyed, investment disrupted, and resources diverted from growth enhancing activities. Civil war, the predominant form of warfare over the past half century, has a particularly devastating impact on poverty and growth.*
>
> *By one estimate, over the past 50 years the typical civil war lasted 7 years cut 2.2 per cent off the projected annual growth rate—at the end of hostilities GDP was 15 per cent lower than it would have otherwise been. A particularly severe civil war can, in the short run, also reduce income per capita in neighbouring states by as much as a third" ……………Civil war and low income go hand in hand. The odds that a civil war will erupt in low income states are 15 times greater than in a developed country. The poorer the country, the greater is the risk of a nation being trapped in a downward spiral of violence and economic decay. A doubling of per capita income can have the risk of civil war. Accordingly, the poorer the country, the stronger the imperative to improve its investment climate to reduce the likelihood of falling into a conflict trap"* (World Development Report 2005).[4]

---

[4] The World Bank, " Stability and Security" in Development Report, (World Bank, 2005), 79   World

On the other hand,

> "*A good investment climate fosters productive private investment—the engine for growth and poverty reduction. It creates opportunities and jobs for people. It expands the variety of goods and services available and reduces their cost, to the benefit of consumers. It supports a sustainable source of tax revenues to fund other important social goals. And many features of a good investment climate—including efficient infrastructure, courts and finance markets—improve the lives of people directly, whether they work or engage in entrepreneurial activities or not. Improving the investment climate – the opportunities and incentives for firms to invest productively create jobs and expand – is the key to sustainable progress in attacking poverty and improving living standards.*" [5]

As such, the unjustified costs, risks and barriers to competition tell heavily upon the tottering and fragile state economy. The economy now suffers two losses of long term nature namely; a) brain drain and b) discouragement to entrepreneurship, which should act as kingpin of development.

To this chapter of discouragement and disincentive, may be added the economic loss created by the so-called Armed Forces Special Power Act, 1958. In order to prevent any further escalation of armed conflict and violent clashes, to restore peace and to aid the civil administration, the paramilitary forces are increasingly used in the Northeast. A vast area is getting deforested for setting up check-posts and cantonments. Besides most of the tourist lodges and other public buildings are occupied by the Armed Forces.

---

[5] Ibid. , P 19

Social Sector

Social sector is important because it is springboard for human capital formation. On social sector we have to pay a heavy price. Most of the educational institutions especially primary, upper primary, high and higher secondary schools cannot run because the buses cannot ply without petrol. For 5 litres of petrol one has to be in the queue of about one kilometer, that too, once in every 7 days. But time is money. As such, the setback suffered by the educational institutions in their teaching - learning programme is fairly high. The students, in the absence of regular teaching programme, can not maintain their calendar and can hardly compete for national opportunities. This rude shock violates the inter-generational equity and deprives the young learners of the right to education.

The non-availability of life saving drugs is another cause of concern. Major operations have to be postponed or avoided. Delivery became a problem. Admission of outdoor patients are restricted. This dismal situation encourages the treatment outside the state at heavy cost.

Institutional Sector

The economic loss is only one side of the story. While most of the economic losses can be repaired and rebuilt, the loss of faith, trust and understanding is very costly. The breakdown of institutions, the loss of credibility and the trauma heaped on the vulnerable population stimulate in the long run a new ground for the bad blood which may take a violent turn on a slightest mistake. This is a long term loss of social capital.

Peace is a "dividend" both in the short and long runs in the sense that the process of value – addition and "creative destruction" is largely shaped by the quality of social peace and stability. In fact, prolonged instability destroys the very foundation of human initiatives and collective endeavour.

Although exact quantifications of the diminishing value of 'Peace-Dividend' in the Northeastern Region has not been made, the region is bound, by and large, to be affected by the vast array of disturbing activities engineered by the so-called organizations of social outfits.

This 'new culture of aggressive social action' in the form of bandhs and blockades on local issues and small pretexts has cascading effects on the growing growth impulses. For example, the greater co-operation and mutual settlement of disputes could have a potential of adding additional benefits to the South Asian countries ranging from $ 80 to $ 125 billion during 1997-2010.[6] This is 'Peace-Dividend'.

The economic impact of conflicts in the Northeast is enormous. This is to be guarded against. Let us remember four pre-requisites (sine-qua-non) of development.

- The will of the people and their preparedness to make sacrifices for the cause of development,

- Political maturity and stability,

- Atmosphere of peace and co-operation, and above all,

- Meticulous planning.

While forecast is a dangerous academic temptation, one can hardly expect a new turn of promising upturn of the existing volatile situation in the state in a near future. Just to quicken the process of incredible development there is a need for sweeping and sustained application of the components of good governance as such (a) extensive participation, (b) rule of law, (c) transparency, (d)responsiveness, (e)consensus – orientation, (f) equity, (g) efficiency, h) accountability and (i) strategic vision.

---

[6] Mahbul ul Haq and Khadija Haq,   (USA: Oxford University
   Press, 1998)

Chart – 1

ECONOMIC IMPACT OF CONFLICTS

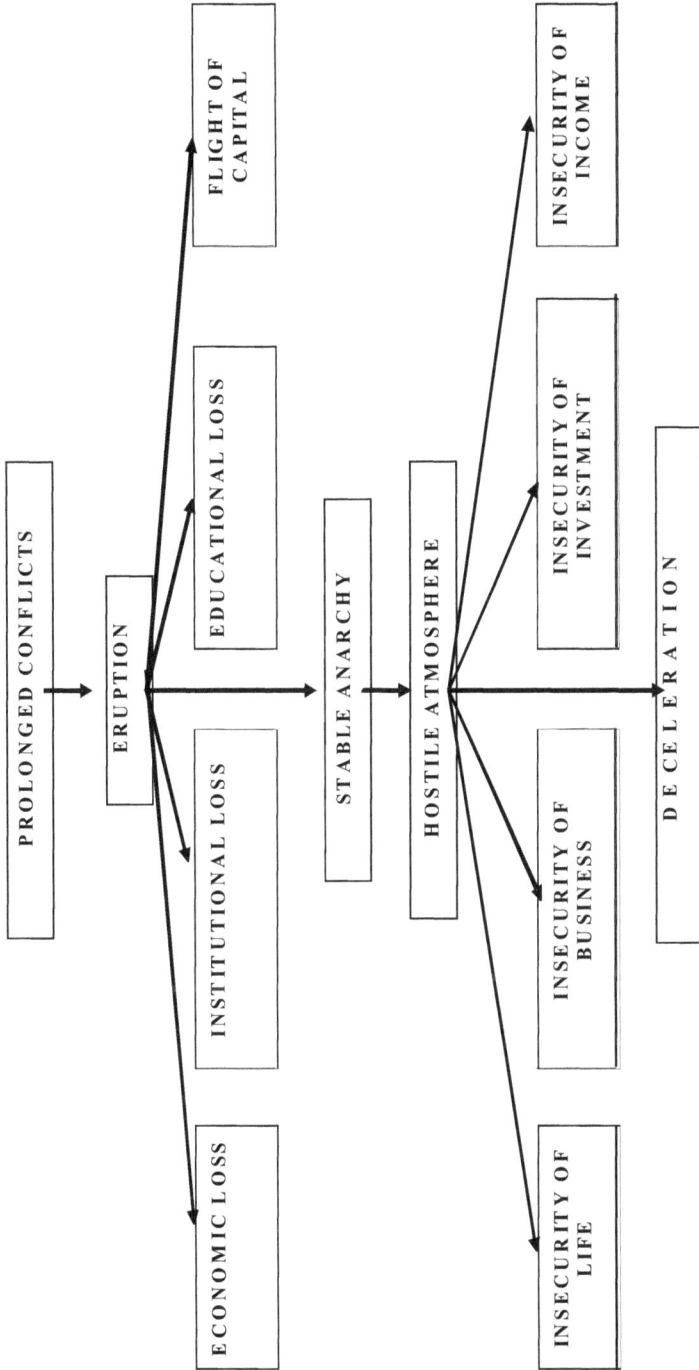

PROLONGED CONFLICTS

ERUPTION

FLIGHT OF CAPITAL

EDUCATIONAL LOSS

INSTITUTIONAL LOSS

ECONOMIC LOSS

STABLE ANARCHY

HOSTILE ATMOSPHERE

INSECURITY OF INCOME

INSECURITY OF INVESTMENT

INSECURITY OF BUSINESS

INSECURITY OF LIFE

DECELERATION

Chart – 2

SOCIO-ECONOMIC DIMENSIONS OF MANIPUR

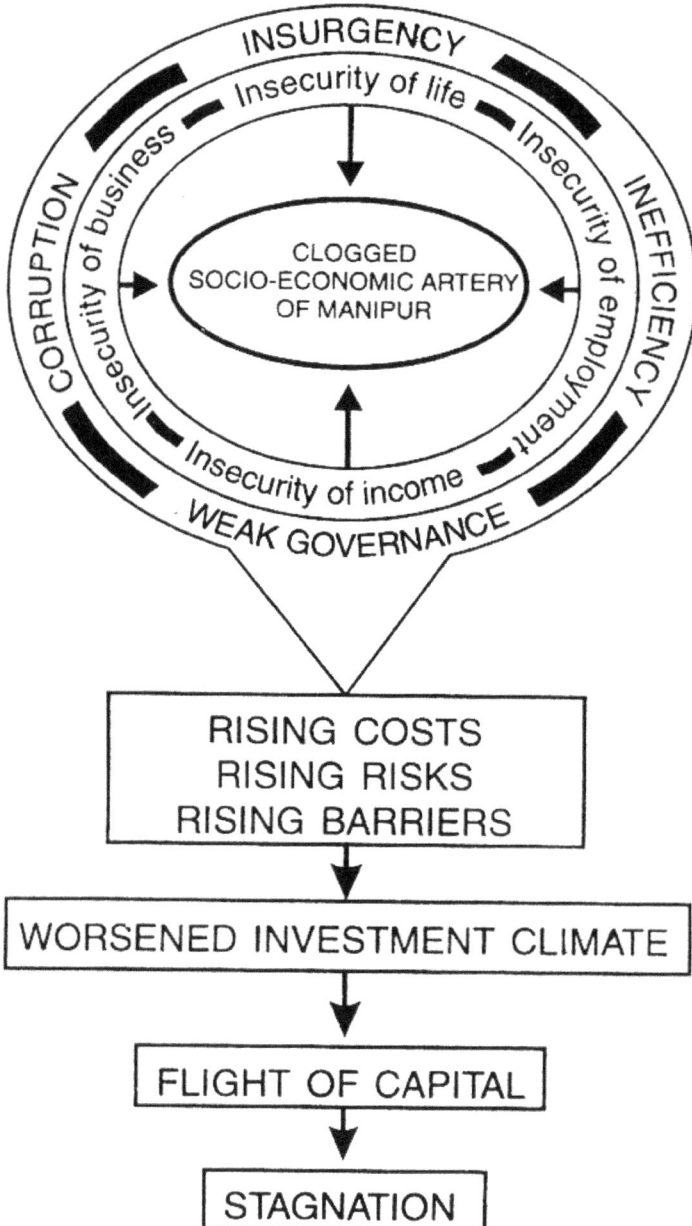

INSURGENCY

Insecurity of life

CORRUPTION

Insecurity of business

Insecurity of employment

Insecurity of income

INEFFICIENCY

CLOGGED
SOCIO-ECONOMIC ARTERY
OF MANIPUR

WEAK GOVERNANCE

RISING COSTS
RISING RISKS
RISING BARRIERS

WORSENED INVESTMENT CLIMATE

FLIGHT OF CAPITAL

STAGNATION

24

ULFA, INDO-BANGLADESH RELATIONS AND BEYOND[1]

Samir Kumar Das

This paper is an attempt at understanding the United Liberation Front of Asom (ULFA) phenomenon - neither in complete isolation from its externalities also including the known framework of Indo-Bangladesh relations nor completely within that framework - but *beyond* either of them. It seeks to tell a story of those forces and processes which are not mediated by any bilateral or for that matter international relations and therefore remain relatively outside the control of any nation-state, and most importantly, how they affect and impinge on both ULFA and the course of Indo-Bangladesh relations. It also makes a call for accordingly reorienting and calibrating India's external policy towards the militants and insurgents of the Northeast.

Much of the literature that has developed on insurgencies and bilateral relations in general and ULFA and Indo-Bangladesh relations in particular has a tendency of viewing insurgency more as a phenomenon mediated, if not determined, by bilateral or even international relations. Insurgencies and terrorism are seen as a foreign policy tool to promote what a state perceives as its national interest. According to this view, the order of nation-states is taken as given and insurgents are considered as too weak to throw their weight around in the fulcrum of international relations in South Asia and constitute a state for themselves. It is for example argued that with the solitary exception of Bangladesh, no state in times of Cold War could be successfully dismembered. Defence and strategic advocacies are

[1] The author thanks Mr. Dileep Chandan and Prof. Veena Sikri for their comments on an earlier draft of the paper. Lapses, if any, are however mine - the author.

accordingly made, taking the present order of nation-states as given and unalterable. As B. M. Jain observes:

"Given the current security environment in the region, India's defence planners require to concentrate more on tackling the Low Intensity Conflicts (LIC) in the form of "sponsored terrorism" by Pakistan across borders. Though all the concerned government agencies are making endeavors both at operational and diplomatic levels to deal with LIC problem, no well integrated approach has yet adequately adopted to thwart Pakistan's evil designs."[2]

As a result, insurgency and terrorism are viewed as the unavoidable evil of international politics as long as there remain nations that are yet to form states and there remain states that contain more than one nation Insurgencies, for instance, continue to be attributed to the divergence between state and nation: "The fault lines between state and the nation is likely to be a basic feature of world politics for the foreseeable future since many states are never going to be able to eradicate the ethnic challenge to their legitimacy and not all nations are going to be able to obtain their own state".[3] As a corollary to this argument, insurgents in the Northeast, in the words of a noted Indian journalist, are caught in 'crossfire' between rivaling nations and states.[4]

As one seeks to understand ULFA's politics in the broader perspective of Indo-Bangladesh relations, one has to guard against this kind of fallacy: Bangladesh, as Taj Hashmi warns, has to guard against the 'India factor' and the main challenge for Bangladesh insofar as Indo-Bangladesh relations are concerned is to tackle the 'India factor' in Bangladesh's foreign policy and relations. As he argues, "Viewing its long-term security interests, Bangladesh should not throw itself into the Indian orbit." He accuses present

---

[2] B.M. Jain "India's Defence Policy in Changing World Order: Contextual Parameters and Conceptual Problematiques." in Ramakant and P L Bhola eds., , (Jaipur Jaipur: RBSA Publishers, 1995), 35.

[3] Alan Ryan, 'Nationalism and Ethnic Conflict' in Brian White, Richard Little and Michael Smith eds., (New York: Palgrave Macmillan, 2005), 152.

[4] Subir Bhaumik, (New Delhi: Lancer, 1996).

Hasina-led government of having condoned India's 'push-back of so-called illegals' (immigrants) into Bangladesh and cultivated the presence of anti-Bangladesh militants in India who demand the so-called 'Swadhin Banga Bhumi' (Independent Bengali Land) to be carved out of Bangladeshi territory for Hindu refugees/immigrants from East Pakistan, presently living in India.[5]

At another level, this approach seems to view insurgency independently of its local roots and any internal basis. As I have already pointed out, it is difficult to believe that insurgencies are planted by 'foreign hands' absolutely from without - although it is perfectly possible that the foreign powers are likely to fish in *already* troubled waters and take advantage of the turmoil once it sets in.[6]

On the other hand, insurgent organizations like ULFA are seen to be so strong to be able to call the shots and influence, if not shape, the course of bilateral relations such as Indo-Bhutan or Indo-Bangladesh or even Indo-Pak relations. Bhutan is considered as too small and albeit powerless a country to crack down on the 'terrorists' taking shelter there. On the other hand, countries like Bangladesh or Pakistan are considered as – to borrow a phrase now made fashionable by the multilateral agencies – 'failed states'. That these insurgents enjoy a free run in these countries, derive diplomatic and military support from the state agencies that deploy them as their foreign policy instruments are cited as sure signs of failure and their inability to exercise control over their own territory and people. Now that there has been a certain loosening of control of the states over the forces and processes (like cheap and unskilled labour, insurgents and terrorists, trafficked women and children, diseases, small arms and drugs so on and so forth) that travel across the state boundaries, thanks to globalization unleashed in the region since the commencement of the 1990s, 'state failure' has become all too appalling and such multilateral agencies as UNDP, World Bank and IMF

---

[5] Taj Hashmi, 'The 'India Factor' in Indo-Bangladesh Relations' in Bdnews24.com, January 22, 2010. http://opinion.bdnews24.com/2010/01/22/the-%E2%80%98india-factor%E2%80%99-in-indo-bangladesh-relations/ accessed on 22 June 2010

[6] Samir Kumar Das, "National Security in the Age of Globalization: A Study of State's Responses to Ethnic Insurgencies in Northeastern India' in Gurnam Singh ed.,
(New Delhi: Kanishka, 2002), 108-27

remain concerned about them. But, 'failure' of the neighbouring states cannot be the reason why it should take a toll on India.

In simple terms, the ULFA phenomenon cannot simply be reduced to the high and low of Indo-Bangladesh relations as much as the latter cannot simply be reduced to the ULFA phenomenon. This has some obvious lessons for us. First, while it is important to understand ULFA's external dynamics, these dynamics in the age of globalization are seen to spill over the given template of nation-states. By all accounts, ULFA's external links have become diversified and what started off as tacit or open support for the insurgents particularly by the neighbouring states is now being increasingly supplemented by transnational and global forces (like the radical Islamist forces) over which nation-states including those that extend support have little or virtually no control. Much of the externality, in other words, has become global. Our external policy towards the insurgents that continues to be directed to state actors will therefore have to be reoriented in recognition of this new reality. Besides, diversification of the external sources has provided ULFA with relative strategic freedom of operation in India. While Bhutan, Myanmar, Bangladesh, Pakistan and lately China are named as potential or actual external base, such a wide base, one must understand, serves as a strategic asset especially at a time when the state and non-state actors in this wide base are not necessarily in unison and India has to invest disproportionately high amount of diplomatic and maybe other resources in order to contain it simply because it affects so many countries. The second section of the paper deals with this question.

Secondly, ULFA is accused of having changed its stand on undocumented immigration from Bangladesh allegedly at the instance of the Government of Bangladesh. It is believed to have reached a secret understanding with the Government of Bangladesh and this ideological dilution was the price that it was asked to pay in order to secure its camps and operations in Bangladesh. Perhaps there is more to it. ULFA's shift in stand way back in 1992 may have exasperated a wide body of people in Assam; but seems to have been propelled by a clear and categorical understanding of the new global reality that migration especially of cheap and unskilled labour across the borders - however unwelcome it may be - proves unstoppable in the age of globalization. While there is demand for it in India, Bangladesh's economy is never short of its supply. The economic logic of labour goes against the political logic of state formation and the sooner the states realize it, the better. The Indian state is yet to recognize what ULFA did in the early 1990s. It is one thing to deny this new global reality and hence to delude ourselves and completely another to initiate a new policy regime of 'work permit' by conferring recognition to it. We discuss the issue of migration in the third section of this paper.

Thirdly, India evidently looks upon the present regime in Bangladesh (along with Bhutan) as an unrecognized – indeed unrecognizable ally in the roadmap to peace with ULFA. Bangladesh plays a crucial role in getting the top ULFA leadership hitherto holed up there to 'surrender' to and work out peace with the Indian authorities. While the instrumentality of Bangladesh can hardly be recognized, India takes utmost caution – with of course varying degree of success - in ensuring that Bangladesh is not seen as playing only an instrumental role in India's scheme of things. India's twin policy of getting Bangladesh to act and forcing the 'arrested' ULFA leadership to enter into peace talks is fraught with danger at least on two counts. One, the policy is intended to split ULFA vertically into 'arrested' leaders who have reportedly expressed their consent to talks and that section of leadership that is still at large and unwilling to come to the negotiating table for whatever reasons. Past experiences show that this piecemeal approach to peace does not pay dividends and sometimes turns out to be counterproductive in so far as it sets off factional feuds, wreaks havoc and hamstrings enduring peace. Two, this approach looks upon peace as a game essentially confined to two otherwise conflicting parties. One has to remember that there are many more stakeholders of peace than are exhausted by the two-party module envisaged here. The ULFA too refuses to recognize these stakeholders beyond a point. As I have argued, the Peoples' Consultative Group set up by it was seen to be too close to ULFA to represent the broader spectrum of the society. Paresh Baruah's (its 'Commander-in-Chief') much-quoted reservations against the recent formation of Sanmilit Jatiya Abhibartan (SJA) and its activities are reflective of his staunch disapproval of any peace initiative that is organized independently outside its auspices. The other stakeholders – whom I broadly described as civil society – become a site of contest between the state on one hand and the insurgents on the other.[7] While the state has hardly any institutional alternative and redesigning to offer as a means of settling the conflict (both the Chief Minister and the Minister of Department of Northeast Region (DONER) recently rejected any talk on the issue of sovereignty without giving any hint of what the Government is prepared to offer), a section of ULFA recognizes only that part of civil society that as it were agrees to serve as its front desk. Nowadays, there seems to have been a shift in ULFA's media policy as well. Earlier it was keen on holding itself accountable to the public opinion articulated and crystallized through media by way of regularly responding to the readers' queries and reflecting on its own policies and activities. Now the policy is to own at least a section of the influential media and thereby try to shape the public opinion. We discuss this troubled road to peace in the fourth section. But we propose to begin with the next section intended primarily to clear the methodological mess that most of the writings on conflict and peace in the Northeast are involved in.

The Methodological Mess

At one level, there has been a glut of publications on the Northeast particularly since the late-1990s for reasons not unknown to us.[8] But at another level, it is also true that very few merit closer attention. The sudden surge in publications could hardly contribute to any significant enrichment of our knowledge of Northeast Studies. Very few of these publications are, to say the least, methodologically informed. The problem is in a large measure methodological. Obviously the data and information we have to rely on while putting across our argument are of extremely delicate and sensitive nature. But in this paper we have depended on only those that are easily available in the public domain and we must confess that we have not been privy to any secret or classified information that are not otherwise shared

---

[7] Samir Kumar Das, , Policy Studies 42. (Washington DC: East-West Center, 2007), available online at http://www.eastwestcenter.org/fileadmin/stored/pdfs/ps042.pdf, accessed on 22 Jun 2010.

[8] Samir Kumar Das, 'Constructing the North-East as a Field: Some Observations' in , XXI (1&2), 1997, 13-33

by and accessible to others. Privileged access to any kind of information and data per se is no virtue of Social Science research, to my mind, even worse - could actually turn out to be more of a liability unless suitably rendered in a language replicable by others. Breaking news is the job the journalists are best meant for and certainly not the social scientists.

Besides, there is the problem of reliability of data and information that are in use. Thus to cite an example, Sengupta and Singh find evidences of 'active support' by state agencies of Bangladesh for insurgents of the Northeast as 'incontrovertible'.[9] On the other hand, Bangladeshi journalists like Taj Hashmi and scholars like Shahedul Anam Khan find Indian involvement in Bangladesh's internal affairs as, much too apparent to require any further proof. Both could be true at the same time; but unfortunately there is very little that we as social scientists can do – to actually sift through the evidences invoked by them and independently check for ourselves whether they are either 'incontrovertible' or 'apparent' as being claimed by them. Social Science evidences are expected to be cast in potentially controvertible or verifiable terms. It is unfortunate to see that many social scientists working on the Northeast allow themselves to be fed by data and information that they cannot independently confirm or verify and not always unwillingly become party to the 'psychological operations' carried out by the conflicting parties. These data and information are far from being innocent and benign.

From International to Global Links

India's relations with Bangladesh in so far as ULFA is concerned seem to have passed through three distinct – though not altogether unrelated – stages: In the first stage, ULFA reportedly started setting up its camps in that country by the end of the 1980s when it was on the run after being banned and the first military operation was launched against it in 1990. Initially it maintained a defensive posture and kept a low profile in a foreign country. It is difficult to believe that Bangladesh did not know anything

9 Dipankar Sengupta & Sudhir Kumar Singh, 'Introduction' in Dipankar Sengupta & Sudhir Kumar Singh eds., . (New Delhi: Authorpress/ Society for the Promotion of Activities for National Development and Nation Building (SPONDAN), 2004), 8.

about its presence; but it clearly decided not to take any notice of it by way of making public statements and thereby publicly acknowledging its presence. Quite the contrary, the Bangladeshi state was in a denial mode as long as ULFA had decided not to become visible.

The public surfacing of ULFA in Bangladesh seems to have begun in the second stage. Once officially banned and sought to be hounded out from India, the organization slowly allowed itself to be deployed as a foreign policy tool of our eastern neighbour. The role of Bangladesh in facilitating its linkage with Pakistan and with the world Islamist forces can hardly be denied. In the bargain, a certain ideological dilution particularly in relation to its stand on the 'illegal' immigration set in by the early 1990s. It will be difficult to conclude – as we will have occasion to see - that this ideological dilution was the only factor responsible for its rapid alienation from the people of Assam.

The third stage is marked by India's policy of taking advantage of the friendly forces in power in the neighbouring countries including Bhutan, Bangladesh and getting them to act against ULFA and such militant organizations as National Democratic Front of Bodoland (NDFB) and Kamatapur Liberation Organization (KLO). But insofar as ULFA continues to harbour and maintain its links with the transnational, radical Islamist forces, its ties with Bangladesh are likely to survive the Bangladeshi State's recent crackdown on ULFA leaders and cadres.

By all accounts, ULFA's camps have been functioning in Bangladesh since 1989 and at that time the number of camps was estimated between 12 and 13. Established initially with the objective of using Bangladesh as a safe haven and training site, the Front gradually expanded its network to include operational control of activities and the receipt and shipment of arms in transit eventually entering India. The Muslim United Liberation Tigers of Assam (MULTA) and Muslim United Liberation Front of Assam (MULFA) are reported to be the chief suppliers of arms for the ULFA through Bangladesh.

It is now apparent that Sheikh Hasina's Awami League Government during her first reign (1995-2000) had asked the insurgent groups to leave the country, much to the relief of New Delhi. Leading a coalition government with a wafer-thin majority that was being constantly held back by other radical Islamist forces and given the invisible rise of these forces in Bangladesh, this was the most that she could do at that time. In fact some outfits like the ULFA, and the National Socialist Council of Nagalim (NSCN) IM reportedly moved their camps to Myanmar. But it soon turned out to be only a relocation of their cadres and infrastructure to newer places within Bangladesh. In October 2001, the Islamists' Party alliance led by Bangladesh Nationalist Party (BNP) won a landslide victory in the eighth parliamentary election. ULFA came back with a vengeance and reestablished its camps at Maijdi, Mymensingh, Rangpur, Mohangaon, Bhairab Bazaar and Pulchari. It also reopened its camps at Adampur, Banugashi, Jyantipur, Jayadevpur, Shrimangal and Cox's Bazar. According to an estimate, by late 2003, 15 militant groups of the region had reportedly been running their 194 camps in Bangladesh.[10]

The BNP government led by Begum Khaleda Zia has been accused of nurturing Pakistan's Inter Services Intelligence (ISI) operatives active in the Northeast, and its help and assistance to insurgencies in the region have been described by some as 'Bangladesh's state policy dictated from Pakistan'. By all evidences, Bangladesh during this time has extended diplomatic support, facilitated their operation in other parts of South Asia and has allowed its territory to be used as conduit for arms supply to be used against India. In January 2010, Bangladesh's Minister of Local Government and Awami League General Secretary Syed Ashraful Islam claimed that there was 'clear evidence' of a meeting having taken place between Pervez Musharraf (former President of Pakistan) and Anup Chetia – the Chairman of ULFA - in 2002. According to him, the meeting, which lasted for about 90 minutes and took place in Musharraf's hotel room, was 'facilitated' by the then Khaleda Zia government.

The Pakistan High Commission in Bangladesh is reported to have arranged for the travel of ULFA leaders to Karachi, from where they were taken to the terrorist training centres by ISI and its affiliates.[11] ULFA seemed

---

[10] 'NE Militants having a free run in Bangladesh',   , 23 December 2003.
[11] "Bangladesh hands over two top ULFA rebels to India" TopNews.in, 11 Aug 2009.

to have paid Pakistan back with full gratitude by announcing its support for that country during the Kargil war. By asking Pakistan, of all countries, for Assam's 'liberation' – bizarre though it may sound - ULFA seemed to have allowed this ideological dilution for military reasons. It again shows how military reason prevails over the political one in ULFA's scheme of things. As Bertil Lintner points out:

> *"ISI may not have been particularly interested in the ULFA's separatist cause, but if militancy increases in the northeast, India would be forced to withdraw troops from the battlefront in Kashmir and send them to Assam, which would suit Pakistan. At least, that was the strategy, as ULFA's Commander-in-Chief Paresh Baruah told this correspondent in Bangkok in March 1992."[12]*

On 2 April 2004, Bangladesh Joint Forces seized 10 truckloads of submachine-guns, AK-47 assault rifles, other firearms and bullets reportedly destined for ULFA hideouts in Northeast India on a tip-off in the largest ever arms haul in an early morning swoop on the Karnaphuli coast in Chittagong. It is believed that at least ten to twenty 26/11-kind attacks could be launched using these arms and ammunition. To put it in another way, it can actually arm a small troop of a few thousand people.[13] *Jane's Intelligence Review* pointed out that the shipment originated from Hong Kong and reached Sittwe in Burma, where the weaponry was transferred to some smaller vessels and shipped again to Chiattagong. The *Review* further stated that the shipment was worth an estimated USD 4.5 to 7 million.[14]

Unlike our Himalayan neighbour Bhutan, Bangladesh has in the past denied the existence of camps inside her territory. The fomentation of insurgency and terrorism in Bangladesh, according to Jafa, is rooted in the very 'logic and history' of her state and society. As he argues:

---

[12] Bertil Lintner, 'ULFA: Rudder-less Rebellions'   , May, 2010. 18,

[13] Diganta, "Was ULFA helped by Bangladesh Officials in Chittagong", The New Horizon, March 24, 2009, http://horizonspeaks.wordpress.com/2009/03/04/ulfa-truck-in-chittagong-helped-by-bangladesh-officials/ accessed on 22 June 2010.

[14] Bertil Lintner, "Northeast India: Boiling Pot of International Rivalry" Yalegobal, 17 Feb 2010

"While Bhutan watched helplessly as the militants' camps were established on its territory ..., the establishment of these camps in Bangladesh was the outcome of a different logic and history that goes back to the assassination of Mujibur Rahman ... and the emergence of an Islamic anti-Indian leadership in Bangladesh. The Islamic anti-India hold on Bangladesh is so strong that during her two terms of prime ministership, Mujib's pro-India daughter Sheikh Hasina could not demolish Indian insurgents' camps which were working under the protection of the Bangladesh army and paramilitary forces."[15]

The caretaker government in 2007 has been, for the first time in the history of Indo-Bangladesh relations, at least willing to listen to Indian complaints in this regard.[16]

But it did not do much in dismantling these camps. It was only with the ascension of Awami League to power with a thumping majority that Bangladesh's regime change could trigger off a shift in its policy towards the insurgents of the Northeast. In the understated words of Bertil Lintner: "... a thaw came with the victory of Awami League in December 2008'[17] and over a year after this Bangladesh had detained several ULFA leaders and handed them over to the Indian authorities.

It is important to note that Bangladesh too accused India of having raised and sponsored Shanti Bahini – the Chakma insurgent outfit - against the Government and fomented the Chakma insurgency: "For Bangladesh, Chakma problem was essentially one of insurgency ... led by the *Shanti Bahini*, which, according to Bangladesh foreign ministry, was aided by and

[15] Vijendra Singh Jafa, 'Insurgencies in North-East India: Dimensions of Accord and Containment' in S. D. Muni ed.,   . (New Delhi: Manohar, 2006), 92.

[16] Anand Kumar, 'Indo-Bangladesh Relations under the Caretaker Government', no. 2266 (June 11, 2007) available online at http:// www.southasiaanalysis.org/%5Cpapers23%5Cpaper2266.html accessed on 22 June 2010.

[17] Bertil Lintner, 'ULFA: Rudder-less Rebellions' in   , 17 May 2010.

trained in India, a charge denied resolutely by India".[18]

As per the reports available in the public domain the radical Islamist organizations play a role in providing arms shipment to ULFA in Bangladesh. Paresh Baruah is reported to have met Osama bin Laden and other al Qaeda leaders through their operatives in Bangladesh. But the Islamist link too suffered a setback when on 27 January 2010, Bangladesh executed five ex-army officers who were convicted of the 1975 murder of the country's independence leader and Sheikh Hasina's father, Sheikh Mujibur Rehman. Among those executed was Lt. Col. Syed Faruque Rahman, who in 1988 reportedly first met ULFA's foreign affairs chief Munim Nobis. There is a distinct possibility that ULFA's link with the transnational, radical Islamist forces might survive the impending severance of its link with the Bangladeshi State. Radical Islamist forces, by all accounts, do not take Sheikh Hasina's moves so kindly.

Her maiden visit to India in early 2010, after she became the prime minister for the second time, was marked by an understanding that neither India nor Bangladesh would allow their territory to be used against the other. While Bangladesh's intentions now can hardly be doubted, it is also important to find out how far Sheikh Hasina's initiatives will be sustainable in the long run and whether it will be within the capacity of the present regime to continue with the same tempo in the foreseeable future. There has been an attempt on her life during her first reign reportedly with an ULFA hand behind it and there was uprising in the ranks of the Bangladesh Rifles and radical Islamist forces have reportedly penetrated deep into the armed forces. The triad of blind religiosity, a significant section of armed forces and a not-too-negligible section of radical political parties (including Jamaat and Khelafat-e-Majlis) and groups are likely to be a stumbling block to Bangladesh's newfound economic progress and political stability. Immediately after her visit in January 2010, I pleaded to India's policy circles for remaining circumspect and cautious in their approach to changes

---

[18] Rekha Saha,   (Calcutta: Minerva, 2000), 183. Also see Shahedul Anam Khan, 'The State and Limits of Counter-Terrorism – II: The Experience of India and Bangladesh' in Imtiaz Ahmed ed., (New Delhi: Manohar, 2006), 162

happening in Bangladesh. As I wrote:

> *"It is important to see how Bangladesh proposes to sustain the tempo of Indo-Bangladesh cooperation that Prime Minster Sheikh Hasina's recent visit seems to have inaugurated. Indo-Bangla relations still have to grapple with a few albeit formidable question marks in future."* [19]

In simple terms, one has to take a more complex and nuanced approach to what was hitherto considered as a simple and linear connection between Bangladeshi and Pakistani States on one hand and the radical Islamist forces on the other. Moreover, if newspaper reports are to be believed, ULFA too is not sitting idle and is now reorienting its policy under the changed circumstances. A change seems to have occurred in respect of its treatment of the media. ULFA now understands the importance of influencing media and civil society according to its own terms. Its earlier approach of holding itself accountable to and respecting the established public opinion of the society by way of regularly responding to readers' queries and comments in the columns of *Budhbar* and *Sadin* has changed to an approach of setting forth the public agenda itself and shaping the terms of public discourse.

ULFA and the Issue of Migration

Although Assam is a standing witness to alarming influx of population from across the borders particularly from Bangladesh, the issue does not form the core of public agenda, for, neither Bangladesh nor ULFA – nor is even the Indian State bothered about the problem. Migration from across the borders dates back to Assam's hoary past. Although the land forms one of the ancient migratory routes cutting across a number of empires and geopolitical regions, it started being perceived as a problem only in the first half of the twentieth century, when the newly emergent Assamese middle class sensing the strain of the migrants on Assam's resources mainly land and employment opportunities, articulated its voice in protest. Immigration of course continued unabated even during the time of East Pakistan (1947-

---

[19] Samir Kumar Das, 'Wrestling with My Shadow: The State and the Immigrant Muslims of Contemporary West Bengal' in Masahiko Togawa and Abhijit Dasgupta eds.,
. New Delhi: Sage, 2010, 54

1971) for a variety of reasons. Much against their wishes, the leaders of Assam's anti-foreigners upsurge (1979-1985) agreed finally to accept the immigrants from East Pakistan till 25 March 1971 – a little before Bangladesh was born as an independent country – through a gradual process. The term 'Bangladeshi' is used currently in Assam to refer to anyone who has migrated from Bangladesh after the country was born and remains illegally settled in Assam.

Bangladesh's response to the question of illegal immigration has so far been two-fold. First, officially Bangladesh continues to follow the same policy of denying that anybody from that country enters or remains illegally in India and that its denial mode continues unabated. One has to recognize immigration as a problem if one were to solve it. Since it pays for Bangladesh to permanently remain in denial mode, it will not be easier on our part to make Bangladesh recognize it. In one of my earlier papers, I actually made a plea for making Bangladesh recognize illegal immigration as a problem.[20]

Secondly and more unofficially, a case is made particularly in scholarly and activist circles in justification of the immigration that has been taking place and some scholars even stretch the point further and claim migration as a 'natural right' for the Bangladeshis. For instance, it is argued that the submergence of the coastal areas of Bangladesh under the sea, thanks to such factors as global warming, environmental disasters and climate change, is responsible for their out-migration to the neighbouring areas of India. Since the factors responsible for this are transnational and global, Bangladesh cannot be asked to bear the entire burden of this and other countries too are obliged to share the burden. Environmental justice in this context is defined as burden sharing. Some even raise the demand for 'lebensraum' and Bangladeshis' 'natural right' to migration.[21] Between these two extremes, there is also the recognition that the figures dished out by Indian agencies

[20] Samir Kumar Das 'Ethnicity and Security in Assam: A Plea for Greater Indo-Bangladesh Partnership' in C. Joshua Thomas ed.,
                    (New Delhi: Akansha/Shillong: Indian Council of Social Science Research, North East regional Centre, 2006), 134-163.

[21] Samir Kumar Das, 'Wrestling with My Shadow: The State and the Immigrant Muslims of Contemporary West Bengal' in Masahiko Togawa and Abhijit Dasgupta eds.,
      , New Delhi: Sage, 2010, 54

are highly exaggerated and many Bangladeshi scholars make fun of it. For example, Shahedul Anam Khan, who teaches at Dhaka University, argues:

"If we take the 20 million illegal Bangladeshi immigrants in India to be accurate, accreting over a period of twenty years, the daily outflow from Bangladesh on the average comes to around 2,000, a staggering figure indeed!"[22]

On the contrary, Bangladesh accuses India of provoking and inciting Hindu refugees and secessionist forces. The Bangladesh Liberation Organization (previously calling itself the Nikhil Banga Nagarik Sangha) functions allegedly with the support of Hindu migrants. It demands the creation of a separate 'homeland' with about 20,000 sq. miles of Bangladeshi territory (comprising Kushtia, Jessore, Faridpur, Khulna, Barishal and Palnakhali) for the 15 million non-Muslim minorities in Bangladesh and also for the 15 million non-Muslim refugees who had been compelled to cross over to India up to 1980.

Although born out of the more militant stream of Assam's anti-foreigners' agitation (1979-1985) targeted mainly though not exclusively against the illegal immigrants from Bangladesh, ULFA gradually looked upon Bangladesh as its dreamland of refuge. ULFA – as we have already seen - has reasons to be grateful to Bangladesh and also to the Bangladeshi State. It returned its gratitude by way of shifting its stand on the Bangladeshi immigration in 1992 – indeed an ideological dilution. ULFA's anti-immigrant stance underwent a complete turnaround by the middle of 1992 when it released an otherwise controversial pamphlet. The pamphlet gratefully remembers the contributions made by the immigrants to different sectors of social life in Assam. It was for instance mentioned that the immigrants have been responsible for rendering the embankments and shifting river islands (popularly known as 'chars') cultivable. It is also unfortunate that they became 'pawns' in the hands of the 'wicked' politicians and are used as 'vote banks'. The document 'considers the people of Bengali ethnic group migrating from

---

[22] Shahedul Anam Khan, 'The State and Limits of Counter-Terrorism – II: The Experience of India and Bangladesh' in   . (New Delhi: Manohar, 2006), 163

East Bengal to Assam as one of the main constituents of the public life of the people of Assam' and redefines 'the Assamese' not merely as the 'Assamese-speaking people' but as 'the veritable mixture of all ethnic groups living in Assam'.[23] The immigrants of the East Bengali origin so far held as potential candidates for expulsion were rechristened as *Asombasi Purbabangeeya Jangoshthi* (East Bengali ethnic community living in Assam). Much of ULFA's subsequent political practice, as we know, harped on the historical and demographic continuities between Assam on one hand and East Bengal/East Pakistan/Bangladesh on the other. If there is history of nation-states in South Asia and international borders that separate them, there is also the contra-history that always opens before us alternative possibilities of remaking and reenacting it. The contra-history thus interrupts the otherwise linear history of nation-states at every moment and imposes on the nation-states the onerous obligation of negotiating and coming to terms with it. All histories of nation-states in the region are closely shadowed and haunted by contra-histories of what could have happened but had never had happened.

Indian State does not seem to have read the writing on the wall excepting that the intelligence community paints a grim and alarmist picture:

The file dated March 13, 2002 (25.1.2002 – NEA – 982) states that infiltration from Bangladesh has altered the demographic pattern of the Northeast. Bangladeshis constitute more than 35 percent of the population in Nowgong (sic), Sonitpur, Darrang, Dhubri, Dibrugarh, Goalpara, Cachar, Barpeta and Nalbari districts of Assam, says the report. They have apparently started to move towards the upper reaches of the Northeast from Tripura and Assam resulting in 135 per cent increase in the Bangladeshi Muslim population in Arunachal Pradesh.[24]

What Indian state has done post Assam Accord 1985 is an open book

---

[23] ULFA, "Asomabasi Purbangeeya janagoshthiloi ULFA-r Ahvan"(in Assamese) [ULFA's Call to the Groups of East Bengal Living in Assam],   (Guwahati), 24 June 1992, 5–6.

[24] Nirmal Jindal, 'Insurgency in Bangladesh: The Role of Bangladesh' in Dipankar Sengupta & Sudhir Kumar Singh eds.,   . (New Delhi: Authorpress/ Society for the Promotion of Activities for National Development and Nation Building (SPONDAN), 2004), 211

for everyone to see and illegal and undocumented immigration continues unabated although, according to some, the pace and tempo may have considerably slowed down in recent years. Immigration is a problem of the people of Assam – not of ULFA, nor of Bangladesh not even of India.

Bangladesh and Peace with ULFA

Indian State's presently followed strategy of dealing with ULFA has been three-fold: (a) securing division-by-division or battalion-by-battalion surrender of ULFA and thereby driving a wedge in ULFA ranks; (b) getting Bangladesh to 'detain' the top ULFA leaders in a discreet manner and push them across the border so that they may be 'arrested' on the Indian soil and (c) promising to let them out of prison only on condition that they accept peace terms.

Barring ULFA's elusive Commander-in-Chief Paresh Baruah, the entire top brass of the outfit is now in jail. The imprisoned leaders include Chairman Arabinda Rajkhowa, Deputy Commander-in-Chief Raju Baruah, self-styled Foreign Secretary Sasha Choudhury, Finance Secretary Chitrabon Hazarika, Cultural Secretary Pranati Deka, and ULFA's political ideologue Bhimkanta Buragohain. Two other leaders - ULFA Vice Chairman Pradip Gogoi and Publicity Chief Mithinga Daimary - are currently out on bail. Now that almost the entire top brass of ULFA is captured, there is much confusion about whether they have 'surrendered' themselves or have been 'arrested'. Official sources, for instance, maintain that Arabinda Rajkhowa and Raju Baruah were arrested only after they had 'surrendered' to them, while they declared themselves in the Chief Judicial Magistrate's (CJM) premises that they had not surrendered and they would never do so. They also asserted that there could not be any dialogue when they were in handcuff. Indian state's strategy of bringing them to the negotiating table by way of exerting force and pressure and treating them as ordinary 'criminals' boomeranged on its face. According to Akhil Ranjan Dutt, this marks the 'critical turn' insofar as people's growing disillusionment with ULFA is concerned. As he argues:

A good number of people gathered in the CJM premises and
some of them openly shouted slogans in favour of ULFA. The

41

*incident in CJM premises suddenly changed the peoples' attitude
to ULFA as far as public utterances were concerned ... People,
who are aware of the facts that ULFA did not and do not really
represent the genuine interest of the people in Assam as the notion
of Independent Assam has not been comprehensively and openly
debated; the map of Assam that ULFA claims to represent is too
fragmented among different ethnic communities; ULFA has been
under the grip of Islamic fundamentalism; and also the act of
indiscriminate killing of common people by ULFA etc. will not,
however, demand that ULFA be treated like very common
criminals. It is for the single reason that ULFA was a product of
specific historical circumstances of a marginalized nationality
within the over-centralized federal polity of India. Common
peoples' opinion on ULFA is very delicate. Common people are
not hardcore supporters of, may be not even sympathetic to ULFA's
violence, but at the same time they continue to perceive the ULFA
cadres as their children.[25]*

In other words, ULFA's 'death' and so-called complete erosion of its
credibility in public eye have been pronounced by many a commentator so
many times since 1992 that one loses count on it.[26] ULFA has died so many
such deaths in the past that today on hindsight it is more accurate to say that
it is like a cat that has nine lives.

Meanwhile, Pradip Gogoi and Mithinga Daimary who were out on bail
met leading personalities of Assam and appealed for their help in furthering
the deadlocked peace process. An 11-member forum called Sanmilit Jatiya
Abhibartan (SJA) comprising academics, writers, retired police and army
officers, rights leaders, and intellectuals, was formed in April 2010 and it
claims the support of at least 100 civil society and other ethnic groups. In
the same month, the Forum held a citizen's conclave and resolved to initiate
peace between the government and the ULFA to put the curtains down to

---

[25] Akhil Ranjan Dutta, 'ULFA Episode at the Crossroads' 2010, unpublished paper.

[26] Thus a commentator observes in 1998: "Today, Assamese insurgent groups find themselves
rejected by their own people and enjoy diminishing external support for their cause" (Sawhny
1998:88).

more than three decades of violent insurgency in Assam. It had sought the release of all jailed ULFA leaders to enable them to hold the outfit's Central Committee meeting to take a decision regarding holding of peace talks with the government. Bolstered by the assurances of the ULFA leaders, Prof. Hiren Gohain who heads the Forum had even claimed that if the government were sincere, then even Paresh Baruah would not object to negotiations. The civil society was also made to believe that the ULFA was ready to climb down from its demand for a sovereign homeland for a respectable settlement of issues. It was also decided that the final decision would be taken by the ULFA's Central Committee. Prof. Gohain has made it crystal clear from the beginning that the Citizens' Forum would not act as a mouthpiece of ULFA as the forum decided to take the initiative as per the wishes of the people for peace. ULFA Vice Chairman Pradip Gogoi was quick in welcoming the move of the Citizens' Forum.

The difference of approaches should not escape our notice. While the Forum wants ULFA to arrive at a considered decision on the issue of peace only after free and thorough discussion and deliberation in the Central Committee - their own body – thereby lending recognition to the decision-making process that ULFA has set for itself, the government seems only too willing to conduct negotiations with battalion commanders, division-level officers and leaders, in short, whoever is captured and could be brought for talks. While for the Forum, respect for the established norms and procedures is the surest gateway to democratic decisions and durable peace, the government is in a hurry to get them to begin talks – no matter whether talks eventually fail. In one of my papers, I argued that continuation of conflict sometimes is even better than failed talks. The history of peace in the Northeast is essentially the history of peace talks with very few of them culminating in peace and durable order.

Two issues, which prove critical for any peace talks to become successful, are – first, the representative character of those who come forward for talks and secondly, a wider debate on and the availability of institutional designs as possible alternatives for conflict settlement. The representative character of those who come forward for talks can only be ascertained through the Central Committee meeting, that is to say, through the same decision-making norms and procedures that ULFA has established for itself and the more these norms and procedures get short-circuited and bypassed, the more their representation is reduced to the vocal and ultimately the coercive power of their claims. The abortive Shillong Accord (1975) serves as a grim reminder as neither of the signing parties was prepared for taking any responsibility for its success or failure. The militants who signed it did it in their individual capacity and the Naga National Council never owned it up. It turned into what I described as 'nobody's communiqué'. [27]

The Centre decided on 17 June, 2010 to start talks with ULFA and formally endorsed the name of former Intelligence Bureau director P.C. Haldar as the interlocutor. "The majority of ULFA leaders favour talks and the government has appointed P.C. Haldar as interlocutor", Chief Minister Tarun Gogoi had said after the talks with Union Home Minister P. Chidambaram.[28] Prime Minister Manmohan Singh met a 6-member delegation from the Citizen's Forum and said that New Delhi has no objection to releasing six top jailed leaders of the outlawed ULFA if that helped in opening peace talks. The government was ready to provide safe passage. The Chief Minister announced safe passage for all second-rung ULFA leaders who were spread outside the country and various parts of Assam. He said: "We want to include the ULFA battalion commanders in the peace process. Most of them have agreed for talks. I am ready to facilitate safe passage". Not all of them are Central Committee members.

Also the government's impatience in conducting negotiations without involving Paresh Baruah – its 'commander-in-chief' – is itself part of the problem. "Paresh Baruah would be marginalized if he remains adamant and fails to respect the voices of the people of Assam," the home secretary said.[29] On the other hand, Paresh Baruah'a appeal to Arabinda Rajkhowa and other leaders who had been detained or arrested by the Indian state to be mindful of the historic struggle of ULFA and not to commit any blunder

---

[27] Samir Kumar Das, 'Nobody's Communique: Ethnic Accords in Northeastern India' in Ranabir Samaddar & Helmut Reifeld eds.,
    (New Delhi: Manohar, /New Delhi: Konrad Adenauer Foundation, 2001), 231-52

[28]"Emissary for ULFA talks"   , Calcutta, 17 June 2010 available online at http://www.telegraphindia.com/1100617/jsp/nation/story_12574913.jsp,

created more confusion and reflected the schism between the two top leaders. Six of Baruah's top guerrilla commanders are still at large: Antou Choudang, Bijoy Chinese, Jiban Moran, Drishti Rajkhowa, Subal Mahanta and Hira Sarania are still in Bangladesh or Myanmar commanding their deep jungle hideouts. Assam's Inspector General of Police (IGP)-Law and Order Bhaskarjyoti Mahanta is candid about the post-crackdown scenario for ULFA: "True they suffered a huge setback but the ULFA killing machine is still largely intact. We need to have those field commanders in our net before we can truly relax".[30]

The Government's newly appointed interlocutor met Arabinda Rajkhowa inside the prison. While he described the meeting as the beginning of peace talks, Rajkhowa staunchly repudiated the claim saying that there were talks between them but certainly not 'peace talks'.

It now appears that ULFA and the Government has been sending signals at cross purposes. While for ULFA as well the Citizens' Forum, the real challenge is to arrive at a settlement – more than simple cessation of hostilities or what is strategic circles is known as 'suspension of operations', the Government is thinking in terms of getting 'the majority of ULFA leaders' to first 'surrender', agree to come forward and sit around the negotiating table. The distinction between peace as settlement and peace as simple cessation of hostilities is only too evident to be recalled here. Is the government thinking in terms of boldly inventing and experimenting with our political institutions as a mean of settling the problem? Is any alternative institutional design of addressing the issue of 'sovereignty' on offer that might lead to the possible settlement of the problem? Bertil Lintner after his recent visit to the Northeast informs: "The word here in Guwahati is that New Delhi may try to neutralize ULFA with money and promises of representation in local administrations – as it has done with other separatist movements in India's north-eastern region".[31] In the absence of any

---

[29] 'ULFA leaders to surrender shortly: Pillai' http://www.zeenews.com/news631835.html updated on Sunday, June 06, 2010, 12:23 IST accessed on 22 June 2010

[30] Bertil Lintner,: 'ULFA: Rudder-less Rebellions'   , 21 May, 2010,

[31] Ibid. 19

alternative institutional design, Assam is bracing for yet another abortive peace accord.

In the face of strong Bangladeshi crackdown, ULFA is likely to stage a homecoming of sorts. Although Paresh Baruah is reported to have hitherto been rather indifferent to the Indian Maoists, his rapprochement with "Indian proletariat" (read Hindi speaking poor people whom ULFA had been slaughtering at regular intervals since the early 1990s) is possible, like the Manipuri insurgents. At home or abroad, it is easier to force peace on ULFA, but difficult to address and resolve the nationality questions that it has raised. In a paper written not quite long ago, I argued that these questions are likely to survive any possible redundancy of ULFA insofar as it ceases to raise them .[32]

Albert and Brock in an interesting paper argue that the relevance of a 'Westphalian State System' as a 'normative world order' has been considerably eroded thanks to the forces and processes of globalization. But they plead for 'retelling' the 'old stories' centring around such foundational concepts as national identity, national borders and national sovereignty & globalization would not constitute a threat to national identity as such but to specific formulations or narratives of this identity. It can be looked at as a new condition under which the old stories about the meaning of belonging to a new nation have to be retold differently.[33] But, 'retelling' the old stories in bold, new ways makes a demand on us for constantly innovating and experimenting with our existing social and political institutions. Institutional solutions can emerge only through an intense public debate. Where is that debate? Who will listen to it?

---

[32] Samir Kumar Das, 'Assam: Insurgency and the Disintegration of Civil Society' in , South Asian Portal for Terrorism, 13, November 2002, 95-116. http://www.satp.org/satporgtp/publication/faultlines/volume13/Article5.htm.

[33] Mathias Albert & Lothar Brock, 'What Keeps Westphalia Together? Normative Differentiation in the Modern System of States' in Mathias Albert, David Jacobson, Yosef Lapid eds., (Minneapolis: University of Minnesota Press, 2001), 46

MIGRATION MANTRA AND THE BANGLADESH NORTHEAST CONUNDRUM

Sanjeeb Kakoty

The phenomenon of human migration is as old as mankind itself. The movement of population, from one part of the world to another, be it in search of food or water, better living conditions or access to resources, at time to avoid war and prosecution or natural catastrophes seems to be an accepted facet of human civilization. However, with the emergence of the modern state systems in which the concept of national sovereignty is immutably linked to territoriality and inviolable borders, the free movement of people across artificially boundary lines has been rendered illegal and mostly undesirable.

Not withstanding the fact of its illegality and desirability or otherwise, human migration continues to be a pressing reality in most parts of the world. As a case in point, one can cite the example of Assam. Interestingly, most of the states of the region were once part of undivided Assam, and share the problem of migration to some extent. But the enactment of strict land laws, the use of the inner line regulations and the reservation of seats in elected bodies for the indigenous tribal population have emerged as strong disincentives to migration to most states excluding Assam and Tripura.

All through the centuries, a combination of factors including geographical, economic and political reasons have rendered Assam a preferred destination for migrations. The fertile land crisscrossed by navigable rivers, abundant rainfall and low man to land ratio ensured that each wave of migrants found space to add a shape and colour to the Mosaic called Assam. Thus one finds Indo-Aryans, Mongoloids, Tibeto-Burmans, Mon Khmers, Tai, Shans, Burmese, Ho's, Mundas, and what have you, contributing their might in the evolution of the Greater Assamese nationality.

To use a much clichéd term, Assam, till recently represented a melting pot of cultures. Past tense is deliberately used to the credit of the processes of modern state building that this melting pot found itself transformed to a festering conundrum spilling over with ethnic identity formation, xenophobia and a vicious cycle of violence and hate. How did this transformation come about? It is one of the most fascinating stories of the use of migration as a tool of economic engineering and later socio-political re-engineering.

This dates back to the British days, and if one were looking at a definite timeline, the Treaty of Yandaboo of 1826 could be reasonably seen as the starting date. Following this treaty, the next few decades proved decisive for the history of the region. By default the British found themselves in a position to exert their supremacy and soon most of the plains of Assam and the surrounding hills were brought under British rule. Supplication of the region brought about remarkable trade benefits for the English traders, many of whom succeeded in gaining monopoly rights. But the subsequent acquisition of the powers and responsibilities of governance brought about the need to maximize revenue collection. This could be done by increasing the number of tax payers or in other words increasing the number of peasants. As happened in the case of Sylhet in the earlier centuries, the British kicked off a policy to encourage migration of landless people from the teeming plains of Bangladesh to the scantily populated fertile plains of the Brahmaputra. How these migrations succeeded in creating a demographic imbalance for the indigenous population were noted in the Census noting of the British administrators notably that of C.S.Mullen. In the early 20's, Mullen decided to raise a discordant note on the issue. He said that though the massive migration of Bangladeshis be credited as being a "marvel of administrative organization on the part of the Government but it is nothing of the kind; the only thing I can compare it is to the mass movement of a large body of ants."

The Census report of 1931 by Mullen was very candid to state that "the immigrant army has almost completed the conquest of Nowgong". It is estimated that between 1921 and 1931 their numbers rose from 300,000 to half a million and by 1936 they owned 36.7% of the land. Mullen went on to make a doomsday forecast that the unabated migrations would destroy the whole structure of Assamese culture and civilization.

But Mullen's prophecy did not goad public opinion towards forcing the government to halting immigration. Instead, the wielding of political power in Assam by the Muslim League between 1937 – 1946 gave a further fillip to the migration from Bangladesh. The stories of the popularization of a slogan "Chalo! Chalo! Assam Chalo! Sonar Mati Dokhol Koro" in Bangladesh and the provision of special trains to ferry new settlers to Assam are part of popular folk traditions today. Probably the icing in the cake was the introduction of a Land Settlement Policy by the ruling Muslim League in 1941, which allowed migrants to settle down in government lands anywhere in Assam.

Interestingly, Sayid Muhammad Sadulla, the then Premier of Assam and a leading Muslim League leader, took a personal interest in encouraging migrations to Assam. He succeeded in dovetailing his policy with the British War Effort and the Grow More Food Campaign, to ostensibly aid the Allied War Effort. In other words, migrations were a necessary adjunct to the War Effort as the new settlers would grow more food!

By the time the country gained independence, the problem had assumed titanic proportions and it was only a matter of time before it hit the iceberg! At the same time, it is true that the government made sporadic and ineffectual efforts to somehow resolve the problem. The first among these ineffectual legislations was the Immigrants (Expulsion form Assam) Act 1950. This toothless act sought to differentiate between Hindu and Muslim migrants. While seeking to treat the Hindu migrants as refugees, the Muslims were to be treated as illegal immigrants. Inspite of this act, the migrations continued and even increased. The 1961 Census report noted the fact the census enumerators were being given false information and it also highlighted the curious fact that while most of the Hindu migrants truthfully recorded their place of birth as East Pakistan, the Muslim migrants claimed to have been born in Assam. Quite clearly, the act of 1950 had spawned its own solutions and migrations continued unabated. As a matter of fact, the communal situation in East Pakistan was prompting Hindu migration in ever increasing numbers and matters reached a flash point with the communal clashes which intensified from 1964, forcing millions of Hindus to seek refuge in India. There is no gainsaying that a vast majority of these found their way to Assam. During this time, the Assam government thought it prudent to bring in a fresh legislation to solve the issue. This Act was ambitiously named Prevention of Infiltration from Pakistan Act. This act tried to introduce a secular element into our law making by doing away with the distinction between Hindu and Muslim immigrants. In addition a special Border Police Force was raised, a total of 159 watch towers on the international border were sanctioned and some six passport checking centres were made operational. It proved to be a case of too little and too late.

The War of 1971 had a tsunami effect on migration to Assam. It is said that the population of Bangladesh before the outbreak of hostilities stood at 75 million. Of these, some 10 million were forced to leave their homes due to the war. On a conservative estimate, it is said that of them, one million never returned home and the migration continues.

Though resistance against immigrations existed in some form or the other, the genesis of a sustained mass movement can be traced to 1979 AASU led mass movement. Six years of upheaval in Assam, saw its reverberations in most of the other Northeastern states. In between, the Centre Government under the leadership of Mrs Indira Gandhi enacted legislation exclusively for the state of Assam called the The Illegal Migrants (Determination by Tribunal) Act (IMDT Act). This legislation was ratified by only one state in the whole of India – Assam. This effectively gave India, probably the only country in the world, the dubious distinction of having two sets of immigration laws for the same country. While the rest of India was governed by the Foreigners Act of 1946, which places the onus of proving ones citizenship on the citizen, the IMDT Act puts the onus on the complainant. This Act continued to mock the justice system of India for a couple of decades before being struck down in the Supreme Court as *ultra vires*. But by then the damage had been done.

The Assam Agitation which had been brought to an end by the Assam Accord of 1985 has remained unimplemented and probably un-implementable.

Land alienation continues unabated and political power is slowly but surely slipping away from the hands of the indigenous people. In the absence of seat reservation, except in those reserved for the tribals, more than 1/3 of the parliamentary and assembly seats have a decisive immigrant vote. The idea of fencing the international border is far from complete and in the absence of proper identification norms for the citizens of the country, there is no fool proof way of weeding out fresh immigrants. If one adds the spectre of fundamentalism gaining a foothold among immigrants, the migration conundrum becomes a potential time bomb.

Add to this the very real probability of a large part of Bangladesh getting inundated, due to rising sea levels to be brought about by global warming. Where would the millions go? Obviously these ecological migrants would be forced to the other parts of the world which would particularly include India and Assam. Are we prepared for this possible deluge? Since Bangladesh alone is not responsible for the rising sea levels but would be among the countries to be hardest hit, the international community owes it to the world to prepare a contingency for such an eventuality. Since, India would suffer spill over effects, and Assam would be a frontier state in this process, it is time for a well thought out, contingency plan.

NONGPOK THONG HANGBA – TOWARDS CULTURAL COLLECTIVES: MANIPUR AND SOUTH-EAST ASIA

N. Vijaylakshmi Brara

Introduction

The spiritual teacher Lourembam Khongnangthaba, an 18th century scholar of Manipur was a champion of Meitei faith[1] who proclaimed that a person who does not know himself, who does not purposely try to know his own individual personality is an *Urit-napangbi* (one who does not listen to anything deliberately, also who does not do anything deliberately). There is no benefit from the presence of such a person who does not know his own father and forefathers.[2] He is considered to be a reincarnation of Apoimacha who was the wisdom teacher of King Khagemba *of* the 16th century. These 'wisdom teachers' never took land or any other tribute from the kings, but at the same time guided the kings on polity and governance. They were ascetics with no worldly desires. 16th century onwards a cycle of such wisdom teachers has been noticed by historians in Manipur.

Three important ascetics of that time, the *Mangang, Khuman* and *Luwang*[3] elders propounded the Meitei religion, associating it with the polity and philosophizing in *Irenba Puari Ahoiron* (The Philosophical treatise of the Universe). From the 17th century onward, intensive debates on the issue

---

[1] The predominant belief system of the Meiteis (The valley populace in Manipur).

[2] Vijaylakshmi Brara,   . (New Delhi: OUP, 1998) 102

[3] These are the three names out of the seven clans of the Meities, the inhabitants of the valley region of Manipur. The others being Khaba-nganba, Chinglei, Angom, and Moirang.

of conversion to Hinduism had started in the *Pombi-pham* (a people's durbar).[4] The 18th century saw a historic turn, when the discourses on conversion to Hinduism received an official stamp from King Pamheiba. He was popularly called Garibniwaz (the messiah of poor). He took a *suo-moto* decision of making Hinduism as state religion, but only after an agreement that after seven generations the old religion shall be revived. This agreement with the king was publicly ritualized with *Nongkhrung Irupa*[5] at the Iril River at Lilong, a town at the outskirts of Imphal, the capital of Manipur. At that place the elders of the seven clans of the Meitei society took a piece of wood called *Nongkhrung* which they sank into the river and promised to confirm to the king and his doctrine of Hinduism with the promise that the old religion will be re-established after seven generations. During the establishment of Hinduism, it is said that Garibniwaz not only burnt the Meitei sacred texts, the *puyas* and razed the temples belonging to the traditional faith, but also went on to destroy the monasteries and pagodas in Burma. He even burnt the Buddhist scriptures.

It is believed that the seven generations ended in the year 1977 and it is since then paving the way for *Nongpok Thong Hangba* (the opening of the eastern door). The myth emphasizes the displeasure and sadness entailing the opening up of the western gates and anticipation at the prediction of the opening of the eastern gates again.

So why then this king who was known to be benevolent to the Muslim slaves, who then gave him this title, and as legends have it, had Naga origins; became such a propagator of Hinduism? One can say that he was furious and tired with the eastern neighbours. His anger was directed towards the recurrent onslaughts by the *Awa* kingdom, as the Manipuri called the Burmese, and hence wanted to close them. The final invasion, of course took place in his son's time between 1819-1826 which was a very bloody conquest and is remembered as *Chahi Taret Kunthakpa* (Seven years devastation).

---

[4] During the times when certain issues needed to have peoples' point of view, the scholars, the nobility and the clan heads, representing the people were gathered in this court to indulge in discourses and debates.

[5] Dipping of Nongkhrup, a kind of wood.

But, then again, why this recent upsurge and a wave towards the revival of the phrase *Nongpok Thong Hangba?* Why does Manipur again want to look towards the east? Why today *Nongpok Thong Hangba* has become part of the hegemonic discourse? One has to realize that wars and human migration in terms of slaves and migrations due to up- rootedness bring some form of cultural assimilation. The constant wars with Burma and also in some smaller way with south China, did bring in misery but along with that it also connected with the social matrix of these regions. Various scholars today are researching the historic diasporic communities in South East Asia, particularly in the realm of slave histories and studying the interplay of the cultural metamorphosis. Conflict in this case then can be seen as building the ground for familiarity and intermingling while the western door was a 'no conflict no peace' zone and hence was also unfamiliar, unknown, alien and therefore perhaps feared and unwanted. In this background, the West, in the form of inroads made by Hinduism is seen as an embodiment of conflict, alienation, imposition and destruction.

Matamgi Khonlgei Thakpa Puya (a sacred text describing the 'journey of time' and recording as well as analyzing the social transformations in the society and the resultant outcomes) has spoken about an apocalyptic vision with the inroads of Hinduism. It has stated that Hinduism disturbed the traditional equilibrium. It talks about environmental damage, flowing of 'falsehood' in the middle stream of the river, it talks about how "cotton fields will start to sink, quarries of stones will fill the landscape, and the person on the fence will come home and eat in 'our' courtyard". It also says that the new generation of people will open the eastern corridors again. *Chingkhei lalumba* (those who reside behind the cliff) will participate in the opening of the eastern door.

According to Terence Chong, the Southeast Asian literature identifies three general historical sources of information. The first among them is through the vehicle of indigenous religions. According to him, "…religion has been a fertile ground for the animation of nationalist sentiments. Religion's indigeneity as a cultural system and its hermeneutical isolation from colonial influence has long provided a conducive space for anti colonialist and nationalist awareness to nurture."[6] The second historical sources of information we get is through the western education. The narrative of the western educated is the post colonial tale of the native who is educated in the ways of the west only to find out that he is not equal to a westerner. The third source of information we get is through social radicals and communists, according to him.

Five centuries later, we are still lamenting the opening of the western gates and hence looking forward to the proclamation of opening up of the eastern gates. The Look East Policy of the Indian government has found a very enthusiastic audience in Manipur mainly because they see in this the resurgence of the legendary *Nongpok Thong Hanba.* Yet, we are still disturbed with the western doors.

Failed Connections

There were various attempts to link the myths of this land with the Hindu epic, the Mahabharata. Arjuna was made the son-in-law of Manipur. Garibniwaz (the 18th century king) asserted this myth by composing a chronicle called '*Bijoy Panchali*' in which he said that this land was earlier known as Arya Nagar, then as Mekhala and then as Manipur[7]. The term used for the death of the person is, "*Vrindavan Prapti*", (received by Vrindavan (Heaven)), and till today, people look towards Puri or Vrindavan[8] for their ultimate salvation. In other words, there were serious attempts to link to the west, but what they got in return was terms like *chinki, nepali, chapta* and excluding them from the general typified notion of being an Indian. Today one can see a renewed interest in researching the old and new revivalists. Followers of Khongnangthaba like Naoriya Phullo[9] who led the religious

---

[6] Terence Chong, "Nationalism in Southeast Asia; Revisiting Kahin, Roff and Anderson", Institute of Southeast Asian Studies (ISEAS), Vol 25 No 1 (April 2010) p.2 available online at http://muse.jhu.edu/journals/sojourn_journal_of_social_issues_ in_southeast_asia/toc/soj.24.1.html accessed on 17 January 17, 2011.

[7] For details refer to Vijaylakshmi Brara, (New Delhi: OUP, 1998)

[8] A major Hindu pilgrimage in Uttar Pradesh state, northern India.

[9] A 1930 scholar whose family migrated to Cachar, now in Assam during the 'seven years devastation' by the Burmese.

revivalist moment in the 1930s is being re-read, re-examined and re-eulogised with not only a religious zeal but also with a nationalistic spirit.

Benedict Anderson explains nationalism through the notion of popular attachment, kinship and cultural bonds by advancing the social construction, even romanticization of the community.[10] The national community is thus imagined not as a specific network of individuals connected to each other in a particular manner but as umbilical cords from individuals to a larger abstract community where everyone was imagined as members in a deep horizontal comradeship. He gave primary importance to culture of symbols, creative imagery and the role of invented traditions as a meta-narrative of the nation. The story of nation is evolved, according to Anderson, through cultural selection as well as through the subjection to the forces of capitalism. Anderson's methodology reminds one of Clifford Geertz who used cultural metaphors to understand the state structure of 19th century Bali.

The legendry "Madjapahit Conquest" ((1343 AD) the armies of the great East Java kingdom of Madjapahit defeated a supernatural monster), which the Balinese see the source of virtually their entire civilization. Whatever scattered elements of genuine historicity this legend may have, the concrete images express the Balinese view of their political development and their pride in the exemplary centre.[11] The collective belief system, therefore is a strong marker of the way nations are built and nationalism is eulogized.

Manipur is rich in written records and has chronicles of the different waves of migrations emanating from or going to the South East Asian regions. Many scholars in Manipur assert that their origins are from the east. Substantiating their argument, they say that most of the migration routes can be traced through the east. Chakpas, the indigenous community of Manipur, have over a period of time spread till south of China. Poireton, the one who introduced fire to this land is said to have come from Burma.[12] The art of preservation of *puyas* (the traditional texts) is the *Han* system,

---

[10] Benedict Anderson.
    (London: Verso, 1991)
[11] Clifford Geertz,   (New York: Basic Books, 1973) , 333

borrowed from the Chinese, *Che* meaning paper and *ya* meaning teeth in Manipuri are Chinese words. The traditional Diaspora of the *meiteis*[13] dating back to 18th century is spread from south west China, particularly from Yunan to Burma. The languages spoken in the north eastern region are part of the Tibeto-Burman, Tai and Mon-Khamer group of languages.

A few years ago, when a team of Manipuri journalists went to Mandalay, they realized that there were several Meitei villages in and around the city. There were Meitei Brahmins, traditional weavers, who were looking for either business opportunities or trying to find their roots. Today, when people of Manipuri origin visit a South East Asian country, they feel connected. They experience familiarity with the dresses, the food habits, the physical looks and the proximity to their own cultural metaphors. None of this is felt when they visit cities like Delhi, Bangalore etc. The disenchantment of opening up of the western door with the inroads made by Hinduism gets more impetus with the widely perceived 'mainland' bias towards the North-east.

It is said that India is a land of myriad identities. But the Mongolian identity which is so clearly defined in the Northeast has not been strongly affirmed as part of this complex land, unlike the Dravidian or North Indian identities, for example. Other cultural categories have been subsumed as 'Indian', but why has the North east region remained exclusive?

Let me quote some responses from the websites to enhance my argument.

"Fifty eight years into India becoming republic on 26th Jan 1950, the entire Northeast India does not picture in what the term 'Indian' - in culture, in principle, in anything in front of the whole world. The vision 'India' as proclaimed by Central Govt. does not include the Northeast India at all, instead the government created a separate 'Northeast India Vision 2020'.

---

[12] Information gathered in course of conversation with the local scholars

[13] The community living in the valley of Manipur

It's the central Indian government which is still alienating the Northeast India from India becoming a single country...Are Northeast Indians not Indians? Or the word 'Indians' to the Northeast Indians a blessing/tagging to identify like household pet? Why Indian government is able to create rest of Indian states/territories to forgo the concept of kingdoms in the past? Why not to the Northeast Indian states? It's time to define what 'India' and 'Indian' refer to?"

People have been disillusioned with the Centre since this state was absorbed into the Indian Union. Geographically, the Northeast is connected to the rest of India through a narrow corridor called the Chicken's Neck. It aptly symbolizes the precarious relation of this region with mainland India.

The departure of the British and the consequent succession by the Indian government was seen by the people as the rise of internal neo-colonialism, "Whatever little power was left with the king... also slipped from his hand when Manipur merged with India [in 1949]. Control over administration came under the supervision of the representatives of the central government and bureaucrats recruited from outside Manipur"[14]. This gave rise to resentment among the people and sowed the seeds of the culture of dissent directed at the new set of state structure and its authority. The inroads made by Hinduism were the first exposure to the ideas of the west and was seen as a threat to the basic social fabric by the intellectuals like Apoimacha in the time since king Khagemba of the 16th century, Khongnangthaba, during King Garibniwaz's time in the 18th century, Naoriya Phullo in the 1930s and is still continuing by various groups even today. The period of colonial rule gave rise to nationalistic aspirations and gave Manipur heroes to remember for all time.

Lastly, the manner in which Manipur was merged with India later became the main planks for unrest and rebellion and personified all that is unknown, unfamiliar and destabilizing. The builders of the Constitution with

[14]Vijaylakshmi Brara,   . (New Delhi: OUP,1998) pp 244-245

the noble intention of letting this region nurture itself, in fact increased the psychological distance between it and the rest of India. The efforts of the State continue to distance us.

An example is to be found in a booklet issued by the Delhi Police "Security tips for Northeast students/visitors in Delhi" in June 2007. It indicates two things: first, that Northeast student and the visitors (outsiders) are categorized as one; secondly, the instructions show an inherent distaste and bias towards the Northeasterners (although the person who drafted the note was a police officer of Arunachal Pradesh). Among other things it says that "Bamboo shoot, Akhuni[15] and other smelly dishes should be prepared without creating ruckus in neighbourhood".

Statements such as this cannot bring the Northeasterners any closer. In fact the psychological linkage with the South East Asia gets reinforced while the differences with India get emphasized.

Sanjib Baruah quotes one student in Kuala Lumpur who had a hard time convincing people that he was an Indian since he didn't "look" like other Indians they knew. On the other hand he was able to melt into the crowd and made friends easily with Chinese and Malays. In Pune, some students, tired of having their Indianness questioned, started saying that they were from Thailand.[16]

Korean Video films: Creating a Cultural Zone

After international border trade was opened in 1994 between India and Burma in Moreh, on the Myanmar-Manipur border, the first wave of goods which flooded the markets of Imphal were a series of Korean films, Korean television serials and Korean drama. The Korean culture was first introduced to Manipuris through a channel Arirang aired by the cable TV Network. Its serials became a hit, cutting across ethnicity, statehood and even 'nationhood'. Language was not a barrier since they were accompanied

---

[15] A Naga dish, made with fermented soybean.
[16] Sanjib Baruah, "India and its North East"   (New Delhi:
   India International Centre) Vol. 32 (2& 3) Winter, 2005, pp. 165-76

with English sub-titles. The popularity of these programmes went beyond the language barrier.

It drew upon a familiar-sounding history, a familiar religion, shared identity, similar gestures, a similar ground for non-verbal communication[17], similar sense of humour, kinship relations, dress codes etc. Otojit Khetrimayum and Victoria Chanu in their paper, 'Mapping Cultural Diffusion: The Case of Korean Wave in North East India' have elucidated the impact of the Korean programmes in this region. 'Hallyu', which means 'Korean Wave' in Chinese, has swept the Northeast. According to Otojit and Victoria, Hallyu has shown a reverse route from the past flow of cultural interchange in the South East Asia. It has not copied or followed the footsteps of Western popular culture, instead it has shown its capability of "cultural creations" befitting Asian sentiments, values and psyche. I have also mentioned[18] that the tendency of the Manipuris even while adopting modern life styles they simultaneously maintain a deep rooted faith in their tradition. "Even while opening up more and more to the outside world these societies are returning to their roots, their culture and their belief systems, informed by an understanding that such a return to the past could help preserve their identities…"[19] Today 'Hallyuwood' rather than Bollywood or Hollywood is impacting the teenagers of this region.

Movies like "The Classic", "Love so Divine", "You are my sunshine" are immensely popular. In the rooms of the young Manipuris, posters of Korean actors have replaced that of Shah Rukh Khan, Priyanka Chopra etc. A teenager excitedly described her favorites[20] in Korean serials: Lee Min Ho, Kim Bum, and Rain.

---

[17] Recently when I met my children's teachers at their school in Tamil Nadu, they asked why the children from our region were so non-communicative? I cited cultural reasons. 'They are not encouraged to be very talkative, especially with the elders. '

[18] Vijaylakshmi Brara.   , (New Delhi: OUP, 1998)

[19] Interview with author.

[20] Ibid.

The Cultural Collective

The historical past with the linkages with the Chinese, Indonesians, the Burmese and the present surge of Korean programmes, opening up of the trade routes with Burma and further interactions due to communication network and increased mobility, the North east of India is coming in the fold of what is called the "cultural collective". This cultural collective goes beyond the political boundaries. The regions of these cultural collective needs to be recognized and the ASEAN need to bring out programmes and policies taking this regional fact into account. The cultural areas need to be mapped out on the map since they remain creative concepts. But these studies will always be at odds with the boundaries of nation-states and perhaps may threaten the patriotic zeal of some people.

A recent book by Jared Diamond, '*Guns, Germs and Steel*', asserts that China with its eight big languages has linguistic links with Vietnam in the east to the Malaya peninsula in the south and to northern India to the west. One of the Chinese languages, the Tai-Kadai family is spread from South China southward into peninsular Thailand and west to Myanmar.[21] He has mapped out the major four language families of China along with South East Asia including Northeast India.

The Look East Policy of the Government of India compelled a serious effort on the minds of policy makers, experts in the social sciences and academic minds to engage in a fresh look into the contemporary social, economic and political problems of these Northeastern states. There is however a genuine neglect of a subject matter of utmost importance, namely the cultural unity and affinity of these regions with those of South East Asia, and other transnational regions like South West China and Bangladesh. This unique relationship in culture-historical experiences of the peoples of Northeast with those of South East Asia has become a subject of genuine importance in the background of the overall drive for economic and political unity with the countries of South East Asia. In other words, the theory and the paradigm of *Nongpok Thong Hangba* has to be explored if we want a

---

[21] Jared Diamond,   (London: Vintage, 2005), pp322-329

better understanding of North-east itself.

Academic studies on South East Asia have predominantly studied the outer influences of Hinduism, Buddhism and Islam from the Asian continent and later about Christianity from the colonial masters. There has not been much work on the indigenous faith, its relevance and its peripheral spreads and linkages with the neighbouring regions.

Although India's Look East policy was seen as an indication of the opening up of the eastern corridors, it is now suspected that it will concentrate only on security issues, which are central to New Delhi, while skirting the areas of cultural unity, which are important to the people.

But, nevertheless there is optimism in the young minds in Manipur, equating the Look East policy to the California Gold Rush of the 19th century.

"There must be peace and development at the most. There is a hearsay in Manipur that there has not been any progress, it finds insurgency and because of insurgency no investments are coming leading to non-development. So it is like a vicious cycle, somewhere we should have to break it," says Oinam Anand in an article in the *Sangai Express* of Imphal. "With the opening of the gate of the East there may be another 'Gold rush' to Manipur from the foreign investor, who knows? It is time for us to prepare and to face the opportunity and the challenges to come. Let this writer not be taken as a man living in an 'Utopia of fools' by those who happen to read this piece after a hundred year or so." [22]

If security concerns remain the prime agenda of the Look East Policy, then the distance will further widen because this part of the region will only be perceived as a geo-strategic area. The Look East Policy, which is being perceived as *Nongpok Thong Hangba* will become the 'Trojan Horse' for the people of this land. Therefore Cultural Collectives need to be further researched and acknowledged.

---

[22] Anand Oinam, "Look East Policy and Manipur",   , 27 Dec 2003.

INTERNAL STRIFE AND EXTERNAL IMPACTS : THE ISSUES OF NAGALAND AND THE NAGAS

Udayon Misra

Today, it would be no exaggeration to say that the Naga "issue" has emerged as one of the most intractable issues before the Indian nation-state, with wide ramifications both within Nagaland as well as in the entire Northeastern region of the country. In this paper, an attempt is being made to trace the changes that have occurred in a movement which began initially with a given sense of homogeneity and a more or less single voice (that of the Naga National Council (NNC)) to its present position characterized by internal strife represented by multiple voices within the movement and claims of territoriality represented by the concept of Nagalim. It is against such a background that the entire Naga peace process and the role of Naga civil society needs to be viewed.

The Naga issue which in its initial stages involved the struggle between the Indian nation-state and the Naga people who were fighting for their "way of life" is today replete with several other important dimensions and top most on the agenda seems to be the question of providing space to the alternate voices within the movement. Hence, the issue of reconciliation among the different factions has become inextricably linked with that of the entire peace process as well as to questions relating to Naga sovereignty and the right of the Nagas to live together under one administrative unit. Any attempt, therefore, to understand the present complexities involved in the Naga struggle must begin taking into account the alternate voices within the Naga movement right from its beginning and the inability of the NNC leadership to resolve the inner contradictions in a spirit of dialogue and democratic discussion.

The initial years (1946 to 1950) of the Naga movement were quite momentous because from the birth of the Naga National Council in February 1946 (re-constituted out of the Naga Hills District Council which had been formed in 1945 at the initiative of the then British Deputy Commissioner Charles Pawsey) till the election of Phizo as President of the NNC in November 1949, one sees the emergence of a consolidated all-Naga consciousness which attempts to go beyond the divide of tribe and clan to forge a common Naga identity, yet the basis of which happened to be the traditional power structures of Naga society.[1] It is significant that the Government of India (GOI) had almost arrived at an agreement with an organization which claimed to represent all the Naga tribes but whose credentials had not been tested in any democratic platform. Nonetheless, the NNC was given the right to control almost every aspect of Naga life ranging from customary laws to ownership of land and taxation.

From this, it appears that at the time of the Hydari Agreement, the Naga National Council considered itself as the sole organization of their country.[2] This was followed by negotiations which the NNC had with the sub-committee on Northeast Frontier Tribal Areas and Assam Excluded and Partially Excluded Areas, when the former demanded an "interim government" for period of ten years with full legislative, judicial and administrative powers. But a deadlock ensued over the ten-year guardianship scheme, which was attempted to be broken by the Hydari Agreement of 1946.[3] Without going into the contentious clause which led to different interpretations by the Government of India and the NNC, it is relevant today is that this was an agreement between the Government of India and the Naga National Council which was by no means a fully representative body of the Nagas at that time. Nor was it in any sense an elected body. Nonetheless, the Naga National Council was accepted by the GOI as the

---

[1] That the NNC would try to build up its organization on the support it received from the tribal village councils would in the long run prove to be one of its major inner contradictions.

[2] Yusoso Yuno,   , (New Delhi: Vivek Publishinh House, 1974), 165.

[3] Udayon Misra,
   (Shimla: Indian Institute of Advanced Studies(IIAS), 2000), 32

66

sole representative authority of the different Naga tribes and it was given the right to control almost every aspect of Naga life ranging from customary laws to ownership of land and taxation. From this, it appears that at the time of the Hydari Agreement, the Naga National Council considered itself as the sole organized voice of the Nagas (with every Naga being assumed to be a member of the NNC) and its decisions were accepted as part of their "national voice".

The Naga National Council, on its part, proved its popular base through the "plebiscite" that it conducted in May –August 1951, followed by the total boycott of the general elections of 1952. Although this period was rightly seen as one of unprecedented consolidation of Naga nationalist forces, yet often overlooked was the fact that there was no unanimity even within the leadership of the NNC on questions related to self-rule, home-rule or independence. No real effort was made by the NNC to resolve these differences and all dissent and disagreement was attempted to be done away with in the name of Naga independence. Perhaps, the entire course of the Naga struggle would have been different if some of these questions were resolved in a democratic manner within the NNC.

The period from the early 1950s till the 1960s saw the consolidation of Naga nationalism and the hegemony of the Phizo-led NNC. The failure of the Hydari Agreement and the marginalization of the moderate voices within the NNC paved the way for the adoption of armed struggle under the leadership of A.Z.Phizo against the Indian State which, in turn, committed the blunder of initially viewing the Naga movement as a law and order problem with secessionist overtones. The excesses committed by the Indian security forces which included the infamous village re-grouping scheme, further helped the NNC to consolidate its position as the sole, unquestioned voice of the Naga people.

It is significant that though the leadership of the NNC was drawn largely from the incipient Naga middle class, yet no threat was posed by it to the traditional leadership of the tribal councils.[4] Rather, Phizo made it a

---

[4]Paul .R. Brass,   , (New Delhi: Sage Publications, 1991), 48.

point to win over the traditional structures of power and this brought him and the NNC immediate gains, though analysts have pointed out that in the long run such a move encouraged the growth of tribalism within the organization.[5] But what needs to be noted at this point is that even as the NNC was consolidating itself as the national organization of the Naga people, there were several alternate voices within the movement, which were either silenced or marginalized. In this connection one may refer to the position adopted by the NNC secretary, T.Sakhrie who was one of the leading statesmen of the Naga struggle. Having consistently argued for Naga independence during the early years, Sakhrie ultimately developed differences with Phizo over the course and content of the struggle and was eliminated on January 20, 1956. Just prior to his abduction and murder, Sakhrie had planned to re-organise the NNC and, along with Jasokie, had called for a general session of the organization on 30 January 1956.

Sakhrie's elimination silenced for the time being the other alternate voices within the Naga movement and paved the way for the armed struggle against the GOI by the newly established Federal Government of Nagaland (March 1956). Although Naga "nationalist" historians have tried to overlook these tensions and have highlighted the united struggle of the emerging Naga nation against the might of the Indian nation-state, yet it certainly began a process of inter-tribe friction, which would ultimately prove quite costly for the entire movement. [6] It is only recently that Sakhrie's role in the Naga struggle has come up for re-valuation[7]

This was also the period of increasing maneuvers on the part of the Indian nation-state which tried to combine repressive legislative measures with attempts to provide some political space in the form of a separate State for the Naga people within the Constitutional parameter. The setting up of the Naga People's Convention (NPC) under the leadership of Dr Imkongliba

---

[5] S.K. Chaube,   , (Calcutta: Orient Longman, 1973), 98

[6] Refer to Phizo's move to occupy Kohima in June 1956 and the virtual withdrawal of support by Kaito Sema. Also see Udayon Misra , "Conflict Timeline" (1946-2007) in Radha Kumar ed.,   (New Delhi:Sage Publications, 2009)

[7] In the course of a discussion on this paper, prominent Naga civil society leader Niketu Iralu pointed out that following Sakhrie's murder, there was a vertical split in the village of Khonoma and that only recently efforts at reconciliation have been bearing fruit.

Ao in 1957 and the subsequent discussions it held with the GOI may be seen as the first major challenge during this period to the hegemony of the NNC as well as the first major assertion of an alternate voice within the Naga movement. The Sixteen Point Agreement leading to the formation of the State of Nagaland and the inauguration of an interim body headed by Imkongliba Ao in February 1961 showed that there were indeed alternate voices within the broad Naga movement which did not subscribe to the politics of armed struggle. But the assassination of Dr Ao just six months later showed that the then leadership of the NNC was not prepared to accept any of these alternate voices.

Nevertheless, the Constitution (Thirteenth Amendment) Act of 1962 was passed which may be said to have expanded the parameters of the Indian nation-state for the first time by incorporating Article 371(A) in the Constitution. This period also marked the first major civil society intervention in the Naga struggle (Peace Mission of 1964) leading to a ceasefire between the GOI and the Naga Federal Government (FGN) as well as the first successful Assembly elections. With this, one may say that the marginalization of the NNC had begun.[8] Though this marginalization has been seen as a fall-out of tribalism within the organization which took on new proportions after parallel structures of power were introduced following the creation of Nagaland State and the introduction of representative democracy, yet one must tale into account the NNC leadership's failure to accommodate alternate voices within the movement, especially after Phizo went into self-exile in 1957.[9]

The nineteen sixties and seventies saw the intensification of rivalries within the movement, especially before and after the Shillong Accord of 1975 which was rejected by a large section of the Naga movement leaders. Although there is general unanimity regarding the surreptitious manner in

---

[8] Udayon Misra,   ,
(Shimla: IIAS, 2000), 46

[9] Although later on the NSCN accused Phizo of being a traitor to the Naga cause by espousing ethno-centric policies and of promoting his tribe above all the others, the fact remains that it was he who had successfully galvanized the different tribes into a nation by giving them a corporate will. His limitation perhaps lay in his inability to give space to other voices within the movement.

which it was brought about by the GOI, yet the fact cannot be overlooked that a certain section within the Naga movement, however small, had opted for a solution within the Indian Constitution.[10] That the Naga movement was made up of multiple voices and that there was no unanimity even over the question of Naga sovereignty may be seen from the course and content of negotiations that followed between representative of Naga groups and the GOI much before the Shillong Accord had been signed.

For instance, during the 1966-67 negotiations with the Indian Prime Minister, Mrs. Gandhi, [11] a section of the underground group including leaders like Kaito Sema and Kughato Sukhai seemed to favour maximum autonomy[12] within the Indian Union. But the FGN continued to insist on full sovereignty, while the Tatar Hoho insisted that there could be no understanding without Phizo's approval. From this it is clear that no attempt was made to accommodate the divergent views within the movement. On the contrary, Kaito Sema was gunned down in Kohima in August 1968, thereby adding to the growing rift between Kaito's supporters and the NNC leadership.[13] This was followed by an unsuccessful attempt on the life of the Nagaland Chief Minister Hokishe Sema (in 1972). Though analysts have attempted to read into this the inter-tribe faultlines in Naga society, it also needs to be stressed that had there been some inner party democracy within the NNC and the FGN, such a situation could perhaps have been avoided. Following the breakdown of the talks with Mrs. Gandhi, the Indo-Naga confrontation took on new overtones with China directly coming into the picture.[14]

---

[10] "Annexure V: Naga Accords: An Instance of Domination through Negotiation" in (New Delhi: Other Media Communications, 2001), 37.

[11] The FGN delegation which met Mrs Gandhi in February 1966 included Kughato Sema and Issak Swu, the present Chairman of the NSCN(I-M).

[12] Mrs Gandhi is said to have proposed that all other subjects other than defence, external affairs, currency and communications be left to the state.

[13] T. Muivah was the General Secretary of the NNC at that time and Mowu Angami was the chief of the Naga army. Kaito was the Defence Minister. Following Kaito's murder, Kaito's Sema supporters set up the Revolutionary Government of Nagaland which ultimately arrived at an understanding with the GOI in 1973, two years before the Shillong Accord.

[14] The ceasefire with the FGN which had been there since 1964 was formally called off by the GOI and the NNC and the FGN were declared illegal under the Unlawful Activities (Prevention)Act of 1967.

After the defeat of the Pakistan Army and the emergence of Bangladesh, the section within the NNC led by T.Muivah and Mowu Angami sought Chinese assistance and the ground was prepared for a split within the NNC. The Shillong Accord of 1975 merely hastened this split, although in years immediately preceding the accord, there were some attempts within the organization to accommodate diverse voices.

The formation of the National Socialist Council of Nagaland (NSCN) in 1980 put a final end to all such efforts, with the NSCN Manifesto declaring Phizo as a spent force, which had turned "treacherous and reactionary". [15] The militaristic structure of the NSCN which was quite different from that of the Naga National Council,[16] left even less scope for alternate voices and it was but inevitable that differences would crop up between the Vice-Chairman S.S. Khaplang and the Chairman and General Secretary of the NSCN. These differences ultimately led to a split in 1988.[17] Ever since then the two factions of the NSCN have been at loggerheads and hundreds of lives have been lost in the turf war between the two groups.

Although initially there was a tendency to dismiss the NSCN (Khaplang) as being set up by the GOI to bring about divisions within the Naga movement, yet over the years this position has substantially changed. Not only has the NSCN (K) survived through the years despite the balance of men and arms being clearly in favour of its rival, it has also succeeded in making its voice heard on several major issues confronting the Naga nation. Moreover, it has been consistently maintaining that lasting peace could be ensured in Nagaland only if all those sections associated actively with the Naga struggle[18] were made part of the peace negotiations with the GOI. Initially, the NSCN (I-M) was prone to dismiss such claims and maintained that it had the sole

---

[15] In its statement of 1984 the NSCN condemned Phizo for promoting tribalism within the Naga movement and exclusively espousing the cause of one particular tribe.

[16] Refer Chapters on the Naga struggle in Udayon Misra, "
", (Shimla: IIAS, 2000).

[17] In April 1988 Khaplang's forces mounted an offensive against the NSCN (I-M) headquarters and several hundred cadres were killed while Muivah and Swu managed to escape.

[18] This includes the NNC/FGN, the NSCN (IM) and the NSCN (K), the Naga Hoho and Naga civil society organisations.

backing of the Naga people to carry on negotiations with New Delhi. But, interestingly, the position which the NSCN (I-M) commanded in the nineteen nineties when its leaders were virtually treated as state guests by New Delhi seems to have undergone certain major changes in the last ten years or so. As the peace talks with the NSCN (I-M) initiated in 1997 continued, alternate voices within the Naga movement continued to make their presence felt and in 2001 New Delhi announced its ceasefire with the NSCN (K) and declared that efforts were being made to include the smaller groups in the peace process.

The question of a unified Nagalim and the ceasefire with then NSCN (I-M) without territorial limits resulted in massive resistance from Manipur and the GOI was forced to withdraw it. Even on the question of Nagalim, the NSCN (K) had its own position. Therefore, the differences between these two groups cannot be dismissed as mere inter-tribe rivalry but must be accepted as the presence of alternate voices in the Naga movement, something which the sympathizers of the NSCN (I-M) are loath to admit. Otherwise, it would be difficult to explain the factional killings of 2003-04 and the intensity of the turf wars between the two factions in 2006-2007[19] which compelled the major civil society groups of Nagaland to initiate a process to stop the fratricidal killings and set up the Forum for Reconciliation in 2008. This was followed by the Covenant of Reconciliation which was signed by the three major groups of the Naga movement. Attempts by Naga civil society groups to draw on the experience of the South African Truth and Reconciliation Commission are also being made.[20] The latest situation arising out of Muivah's attempt to visit his home village of Somdal in Manipur and the subsequent blockade have united an overwhelming majority of the Nagas both in Nagaland and Manipur on ethno-nationalist lines. But, it is significant that even within this expression of solidarity, there have been

---

[19] Sashinungla, "Nagaland: Insurgency and Factional Intransigence",   , Institute of Conflict Management, New Delhi available online on http://www.satp.org/satporgtp/publication/faultlines/volume16/Article4.htm

[20] Kesheli Chishi, "My Experience with the Naga Peace Initiative: Women Activists and Conflict" in   Vol II, (Guwahati: Cotton College Women's Forum, 2010).

dissenting voices[21] which indicate the presence of a democratic framework within Naga society which is not necessarily reflected in the structure of the militant outfits.

In a rather belated acknowledgement of the presence of such alternate voices, Muivah has recently stated that he is willing to meet S.S. Khaplang and work towards reconciliation. However, it would be wrong on Muivah's part if he thought that reconciliation meant the acceptance of the NCSN (I-M) viewpoint.[22] The question of first arriving at territorial unification before a "political" solution is worked out has also been questioned by certain Naga voices. In the light of all this, it is evident that the issue of Naga sovereignty has now been marginalized somewhat by the issue of territorial unification and reconciliation. Till recently, however, the two most important issues posed by the Naga movement have been the question of Naga sovereignty/self-determination and the question of a unified Nagalim/Greater Nagalim.[23] To this has now been added the question of reconciliation among the different segments of the Naga movement.

While the issue of a unified Nagalim is bound to face insurmountable hurdles in the form of opposition from the neighbouring states and would also involve the changing of existing state boundaries under the provisions of Articles 2-3 of the Constitution of India, it is also bound to create problems for the Naga populations residing in these states. The public response in other states to the blockade of Manipur showed, among other things, that the sympathies of the peoples of the neighbouring states lay largely with the people of Manipur. This, in turn, is bound to affect New Delhi's perception of the problem, all its dilly-dallying notwithstanding. What is further important

---

[21] Refer statement made by NSCN (K) leaders including Khaplang regarding Muivah's proposed visit as well as on the question of greater Nagalim.

[22] Refer to NSCN(K) statement published in   , Guwahati, June 7, 2010, which offers a sharp critique of the position adopted by NSCN(I-M) as well as some civil society bodies and questions the right of Th Muivah to represent all the Nagas. Also see, "NSCN-K against Muivah's visit to Sumi area", The Assam Tribune, June 22, 2010, for report on Sumi Hoho's stand on the issue. available at http://www.assamtribune.com/scripts/detailsnew.asp?id=jun2210/oth06, accessed on 27 July 2011

[23]Udayon Misra, "Towards a Resolution of the Naga Issue" in Monirul Hussain ed.,
                        ,(New Delhi: New Delhi: Regency Publications, 2005),160-169.

is that the insistence on a unified Nagalim is bound to eat into the common struggle and solidarity of the people's of the northeastern region for a truly federal relationship with the Indian Union. As for the all-important issue of Naga reconciliation, it needs to be remembered that historically, it is beyond the imagination of the different Naga tribes to totally merge or surrender their identities in what may be termed as the greater fabric of Naga nationalism. The in-built autonomy/self-governance of each tribe is as unique a part of the Naga historical tradition as is the stated uniqueness of the Nagas as a whole. Any attempt, therefore, to reduce this autonomy in the name of a wider and more encompassing Naga national identity is bound to meet with different degrees of resistance.[24]

Therefore, any process of national reconciliation would have to involve the acceptance of alternate voices within the broader Naga movement. This is exactly where one feels that the leaders of the different streams of the Naga movement have not been able to create the necessary spaces for viable democratic functioning and transparency. Any national movement which fails to accommodate the divergent views and which lacks the capacity for self-criticism and democratic functioning marked by inner-party debate invariably ends up in a cul-de-sac of contradictions which prove increasingly difficult to resolve. This is all the more true of the Naga movement which began as a move to bring together the different warring tribes on a united national platform to fight a common enemy which it felt was posing a threat to the identity and culture of the Naga people as a whole. The attempts to present a consolidated national platform by referring to the "unique" history of the Nagas and their right to live under a common territorial unit have not been successful precisely because of the clan/tribe based structure of Naga society.

When one refers to the unique history of the Naga people as emphasized time and again by the NSCN(I-M) during its negotiations with the GOI, it also needs to be remembered that these very uniqueness draws its strength from the autonomous character of village/clan/tribe functioning on which

---

[24] "NSCN-K against Muivah's visit to Sumi area", , Guwahati June 22, 2010, available at http://www.assamtribune.com/scripts/detailsnew.asp?id=jun2210/oth06, accessed on 27 July 2011

the traditional structures of power revolve. Therefore, to see it from another angle, the very appeal of a consolidated, unified Naga national identity would eventually depend on how well it would be able to accommodate these unique autonomous structures that exist within Naga society. Thus, the very uniqueness can be at times a challenge to the idea of a common Naga national identity. That is exactly why the present process of reconciliation within the Naga movement has taken on such important overtones. It is the internal contradictions within the Naga movement that need to be seriously addressed at the present juncture and the outcome of the peace negotiations as well as the question of a unified Nagalim hinges on this. The process of alienation of certain segments within the movement which started in the late 1950s has reached such a point today that the need for reconciliation and unity within the movement seems to override all other factors.

RAMIFICATION OF CONFLICTS IN TRIPURA AND MIZORAM

Jayanta Bhattacharya

The greatest human migration in history- the partition of the Indian subcontinent into India and Pakistan – saw the movement of more than fifteen million people. This massive displacement forced extensive and well-documented suffering and brought about major socio-economic and political changes. Tripura, a princely state bordered on three sides by then East Pakistan (now Bangladesh), was most affected by migration. Partition opened the floodgates to migrants who outnumbered the indigenous people of the state. Within a decade, the partition permanently changed the demography of the state.

This paper points out how the tribes of the state were marginalized in terms of possession of land, profession and identity culminating in a conflict between the Hindu Bengali migrants and the tribal groups of the state and its consequences.

Tripura, once ruled by tribal kings of the Manikya dynasty with tribals constituting the majority among their subjects, merged with India officially on October 15 1949. According to the 1941 census, tribals constituted 53.16 per cent of the population; in just ten years that figure fell to 37.23 per cent. The demographic change paved the way for the eventual conflict between the tribals and Bengali migrants which devastated the state for more than three decades. In addition, the independence of India led to Tripura's geographical isolation from the 'mainland' creating major hurdles to economic development, especially communications and transport since all goods and travelers had to move by a circuitous route bypassing East Pakistan to reach the "mainland."

During pre-partition days, the king of Tripura had complete sway over his hilly domain (roughly the present geographical area of Tripura) and, in addition, had a Zamindari (land tenure) in 'Chakla Roshanabad' comprising four districts of present-day Bangladesh, then East Bengal and later East Pakistan, such as Comilla, Noakhali, Chittagong and parts of Sylhet. Many Bengalis were thus subjects or tenants of successive Tripura kings.

The Tripura kings encouraged Bengali migration into the interior areas of the state for their own interests. As attested by the 'Rajmala', Tripura's royal chronicles, they had always placed educated and trained Bengalis in high positions to modernize the royal administration; they also encouraged settlement of Bengali peasants with incentives such as land grants. The reasons were two fold – augmentation of revenue and persuading the tribals, who were mostly jhum or 'shifting' cultivators, to take to settled cultivation. The first Imperial census conducted by the British government in 1871 put the Bengali population in Tripura at 30 per cent, a figure that grew slowly and steadily.

However, the realization had dawned on King Bir Bikram Kishore Manikya (1923-1947), that his tribal subjects could ultimately be swamped by the Bengali influx, prompting him to create a tribal reserve in 1943 encompassing 2050 sq miles of land, meant for the Tripuri, Reang Halam, Noatia and Jamatiya tribes. They were known as 'Pancha Tripuri' and his far-sightedness was reflected in the fact that this tribal reserve was the precursor of the present Tripura Tribal Areas Autonomous District Council (TTAADC).

Within three decades of partition, the tribes were reduced to less than 30 per cent of the state's population completely marginalizing them in politics, economy, and control of land. The influx intensified the process of land alienation from the tribal people and added to their collective sense of loss and marginalization.

Subsequent to the merger of princely state of Tripura with the Indian Union at the time of Indian Independence, land alienation of the tribals emerged as a major problem. Between 1947 and 1971, altogether 6, 09,998 Bengalis, displaced from East Pakistan, came to Tripura for rehabilitation and resettlement. Since the total population of the state in 1951 was 6, 45,707, it is not difficult to imagine the tectonic population pressure created on the tiny state. In this period, the state government settled the refugees on land under different schemes, enabling them either to get financial assistance or helping them to buy land.

The implementation of these schemes speeded up the process of large-scale loss of tribal lands. The tribals continued to be impoverished, reflected in the increase in the number of tribal agricultural labourers in the three decades since the partition. In 1951, cultivators constituted 62.94 per cent of the total tribal workforce in the state, while only 8.93 per cent were in the category of agricultural labourers. But in 1981, the percentage of farmers in the tribal workforce had fallen to 43.57 per cent while the number of agricultural laborers had risen to 23.91 per cent.

Growing land alienation has remained a recurrent theme in tribal militancy since it first surfaced with the 'Sengkrak' (Clenched Fist) movement in the mid-1960s. The opening up of much of the Tribal Reserve Area for refugee settlement by the Congress government of post-princely Tripura added to the existential problems of the tribal community.

In 1952, the legendary Communist leader Dasarath Deb, then a Member of Parliament, had drawn the attention of Prime Minister Jawaharlal Nehru to the continuous influx from East Pakistan, suggesting reservation of more areas of Tripura for tribals.

In 1955, Indian Home Affairs Minister Govind Ballabh Pant expressed a similar opinion, favouring new tribal land reserves. In 1960, the Chief Commissioner of Tripura, N. M. Patnaik, represented before the U. N. Dhebar Commission,[1] that specific areas of the state should be declared as reserves for the tribals under the Fifth Schedule of the Constitution. But the Dhebar Commission suggested that special tribal development blocks in

---

[1] A commission known as the Schedule Areas and Schedule Tribes was formed under the Chairmanship of UN Dhebar on 28 April 1960.

tribal compact areas be created first and the Fifth Schedule could be tried if the experiment on tribal development blocks failed.

But little was done to protect tribal rights on lands. In order to consolidate its refugee vote bank, the Congress government continued to encourage the settlement of migrants from East Pakistan. In some areas of Tripura, the refugees formed co-operatives like the Swasti Samity and took to extensive land grabbing in tribal compact areas, undermining and ensuring the failure of the Dhebar Commission's own proposal. Before Tripura became a state, the Communists had won both the Parliament seats in the state. They advocated limited autonomy and the creation of a tribal reserve to protect tribal lands.

But the state unit of the Congress, dominated by Bengali refugees, was determined to take advantage of Tripura's changing demography and ride to power on the strength of its newly acquired refugee vote banks. In 1967, the Communist Party lost both Parliament seats to the Congress for the first time in Tripura. That year, an exclusively tribal-based political party 'Tripura Upajaty Juba Samity' (Tripura Tribal Youth League) or the TUJS was formed. The same year, the first tribal insurgent group, Sengkrak, surfaced in North Tripura.

Four years later, Tripura became a full-fledged state[2] along with Manipur as part of the process of the second reorganization of the Northeastern region. The movement for tribal autonomy continued to gain momentum and three primary reasons fuelled the campaign:-

- Since 1967, ethnicity began to shape Tripura's politics in a more pronounced manner than ever before as the TUJS and the Sengkrak began to focus on the marginalization of the tribals in their homeland as their major political theme,

- The Communists, challenged by the TUJS in their tribal base and accused of failing to protect the interests of the indigenous people, lent their support to the ethno-centric political demands for tribal

---

[2] With reorganization of the state on 1 September 1956, Tripura became a Union Territory. Tripura became a full fledged state on 21 January 1972.

autonomy,

- The Central government saw the grant of autonomy as a way out to curb growing tribal militancy in Tripura and also in other parts of the Northeast.

The Congress was voted out in 1978, following a nationwide trend that reflected a public backlash after the authoritarian state of Internal Emergency (1975 to1977) and the Communists, now more acceptable amongst Bengalis than amongst the tribes, came to power in the state assembly for the first time with a thumping majority. Strangely, in December 1978, the remnants of the now-defunct Sengkrak and the militant elements of the TUJS combined to form the underground Tribal National Volunteers (TNV) to fight for "Swadhin Tripura" (independent Tripura). The extremist challenge and the growing pressure of the TUJS prompted the Communists to push for tribal autonomy with backing from the new anti-Congress dispensation in Delhi.

The Tribal Areas Autonomous District Council was created by an Act of Parliament in 1979, and brought under the Sixth Schedule. A Leftist juggernaut has steamrolled all political opposition and ruled the state virtually unchallenged, except for a brief period in the late 1980s, However, in June 1980, Tripura was rocked by unprecedented ethnic riots, disrupting the whole process of implementing the autonomy provisions. It was only in January 1982, that the elections to the newly formed Council could be held and the Council be constituted.

Underground politics also played an important role with one group claiming greater rights of representation over others, divided by tribal barriers and mobilization. Thus, after the TNV surrendered, two other insurgent groups were formed, each with a different agenda — the All Tripura Tiger Force (ATTF) and National Liberation Front of Tripura (NLFT). While the NLFT gave slogans for 'Free Tripura' the ATTF raised the demand of deportation of Bengalis whose names did not figure in the electoral rolls of 1952.

The demographic imbalance in Tripura spawned by the influx of Bengali

Hindu settlers from the then East Pakistan (now Bangladesh) carried the seeds of ethnic conflict. The state witnessed the Mandai massacre on 8 June 1980 in which nearly 350 settlers were butchered within a span of four hours, their houses burnt and belongings looted.

This massacre was followed by severe riots in which more than 1,000 people including tribals died. The tribals and Bengalis had lived in the state for long time in peace and tranquility, but the riots and growing ethnic division broke the bond of mutual trust. More than 6000 Bengalis have died in violence unleashed by different rebel groups over the last 25 years, more than 1000 have been kidnapped (many were released after payment of large ransoms that pauperized the families of the victims).

Repeated ruthless attacks by armed insurgents on the Bengali settlers mostly living in the tribal council areas or at the fringe of the council areas led to huge displacement. Revenue Minister Keshab Majumder in a statement to the State Assembly on January 13, 2006 said that during the last five years at least 1, 24,000 people, mostly Bengali farmers were displaced in insurgency related violence. The opposition Congress says that this is an under-estimate and that in the last 12 years alone, more than three lakh non-tribal people were displaced.

The US Committee for Refugees estimates the displacement of Bengalis in Tripura at more than 200,000.[3]

A large number of tribals living in hilly and interior areas, mostly in district council areas were also displaced due to insurgency. They faced extortion and threats, including selective killing depending on their political loyalties. Since the NLFT targeted the activists and supporters of the ruling CPI-M, the state government rehabilitated them in cluster villages near the main roads, provided security cover, distributed doles, constructed makeshift houses, gave healthcare, drinking water facilities, education etc. But their displacement let to a growth of alienation from their traditional social systems.

Thus, during the violent years, the schools, primary health centers and

---

[3] US Committee for Refugees, Special Report on Northeast India, compiled by Hiram Ruiz, 2000.

most of the government offices were closed; teachers and doctors did not go to their work places out of fear. This in turn led to an increase in the rate of school dropouts and near total collapse of the health care system.

The tribals also faced the problems of insurgency partly because the Bengalis living in the tribal council areas were targeted by the insurgents, who had bases in neighbouring Bangladesh. Taking advantage of easy transborder crossing, the rebels attacked the densely inhabited Bengali villages near the Indo-Bangla international border. The ultras made the council areas their bastion and operated there. They easily could sneak into the neighbouring Bangladesh, which has 856 km long borders with Tripura. There were at least 30 camps in Chittagong Hill Tracts (CHT), Sylhet and Moulavi Bazar districts. So, it was not possible to contain the insurgency merely by augmenting forces, intensifying patrolling and launching major offensive against the guerrillas, who were expert in bush wars. They forced people to pay taxes, abducted them for ransom and killed innocents to instill fear and sharpen the ethnic divide.

The Bengalis abandoned many of the villages on the border and took shelter in less vulnerable areas in other parts of the state. The security forces in retaliation would attack tribal groups and settlements. The tribal people were thus sandwiched by the conflict between two armed groups – insurgents and security forces.

A Success Story

Yet, over recent years, the state has witnessed massive changes, from conflict to tranquility. The riots, ethnic conflicts and massacres appear to be a thing of the past. The schools in the hills are full of children again, vacated by the security forces. The doors of Government offices and banks were open to the public. The Primary Health Centers (PHC) which had not seen doctors for years are manned once again. And although the old relationship is not re-established, trust is being re-established between the plains and hill people. Things began to change with a combination of political firmness, stringent security measures and determined development efforts. The key has been the state government's pro-activeness.

The Autonomous District Council (ADC) for tribals constitute two third of the state's territory and is the home to the tribes who form one-third of the population.

A multi-pronged strategy was worked out: first, the security forces and their anti-insurgency operations, especially local police, benefited from a massive modernization drive, with officers and lower ranks being provided modern weapons, equipment for swift communications, advanced training in jungle warfare and deployment in strategic locations to prevent movement of the militants.

Second, the Central government, in association with the state government, developed a rehabilitation package for surrendered insurgents; this helped to bring back what local politicians called "misguided youths to the mainstream". Thus, the Chief Minister, Manik Sarkar, was able to tell the State Assembly on June 15, 2010 that "as many as 7,992 insurgents of different outfits including the outlawed National Liberation Front of Tripura (NLFT) and All Tripura Tiger Force (ATTF) have surrendered to the authorities in last 17 years." The graph of insurgency-related violence dropped rapidly. In 2009-10, as many as 225 insurgents surrendered and during this period, the number of insurgency related incidents fell to 24 in which nine persons died. The number of insurgency related incidents in 2007 was 113 which came down to 80 in 2008.

A major reason for the sudden drop in violence must be credited to the Bangladesh government which has taken action against the insurgents located there, breaking up the camps and handing over the rebels to Indian authorities. With the Awami League Government (of Bangladesh Prime Minister Sheikh Hasina) coming back to power, the situation started changing. Harbouring of the insurgents stopped and the ultras were either being handed over to Indian authority or pushed back. Surrender of the huge number of ultras from their base camps was the fallout of the proactive measures taken by the Bangladesh government, Sheikh Hasina's visit to Delhi last January was a significant milestone in paving the ways for restoring the spirit of brotherhood and close co-operation between the two countries.

In addition, connectitivity with Bangladesh has improved with new road and railway lines being opened up and access to Chittagong Port, a long-standing Indian demand, also being provided. Under the terms of an agreement, India has to develop the rail and road connections to the port from Tripura and also re-develop and dredge Chittagong, one of the best sea ports of South Asia.

The conflict in Tripura is basically over the loss of tribal lands, sharing of powers and subsequent pauperization of the tribals. The government decided that the challenge of land alienation could be reduced by giving land holdings to the tribal in forest areas, which constitute 60 per cent of the state's territory.

That good implementation and good governance is good politics, is seen in the results of the elections for the Tripura Tribal Areas Autonomous District Council (TTAADC) which were held on May 3, 2010. The Left Front made a clean sweep of all 28 elective seat, further consolidating its traditional base among the indigenous people, with 63.80 per cent of the votes, brushing aside the Congress and its former poll ally, the Indigenous Nationalist Party of Tripura (NLFT), headed by Bijoy Hrankhawl, an insurgent-turned political leader..

Conflict in Mizoram

Another example of the different aspects of conflict resonates from the neighbouring state of Mizoram, where insurgency began with the infamous Mautam Famine[4] of the 1960s and ended with the Mizo Peace Accord of 1986. In the latter, the former insurgent leaders were absorbed

---

[4] Bamboo forests account for a large portion of the forested area of Mizoram. When bamboo plants flower after every fifty years in what is locally known as the Mautam, they produce a large volume of seeds, which are rich with protein and used as food by rats. Consuming the protein-rich seeds, the rats proliferate and armies of these marauding rodents destroy agricultural crops and stored grain. The Mizo insurgency can be attributed substantially to the inept handling of the famine by the then Assam Government. The present Mizoram was the Lushai Hills district under Assam at the time. The famine claimed 10,000 to 15,000 lives. In February, 1966, an ethnic separatist organization called the Mizo National Front (MNF) almost overran the entire district in a series of simultaneous surprise attacks and captured even much of Aizawl, its capital. The MNF was earlier known as the Mizo National Famine

into the politics of the State, and following that, the State has remained largely peaceful, barring peripheral conflicts.

It is these conflicts that we wish to review here briefly for they reflect a large discord – that while many insurgencies are accommodated by the Indian State, there are many "smaller" problems which are overlooked in the rush for settlement with the larger group. In time, these issues fester and break out into little rebellions and insurgencies of their own, frustrated by the lack of response from the larger community and the lack of interest in New Delhi.

Prominent among them have been the Brus or Reangs, who were forced out of the State into neighbouring Tripura in 1997, following alleged atrocities. Nearly 17,000 of them, whose number steadily grew to about 35,000 by early 2000, were housed in six relief camps in the Kanchanpur sub-division of North district in Tripura. As Mizoram government dithered over the repatriation of the Reangs, citing reasons like an inflated number of refugees, militant outfits like the Bru National Liberation Front (BNLF) and subsequently, Bru Liberation Front of Mizoram (BLFM) emerged out of the camps and indulged in intermittent violence inside Mizoram and also in the border areas in Assam. Other organizations like the Hmar People's Convention-Democracy (HPC-D), however, continue to carry out its activities beyond the borders of Mizoram, mostly inside Assam and Manipur.

Front (MNFF) but the group dropped the word famine and a new political organization was formed on October 22, under the leadership of Laldenga with the specific goal of achieving independence from India. With the active support of neighbouring Pakistan the MNF formed a trained army and attacked the Indian installations with sophisticated weapons on February 28, 1966. They attacked Government offices and Assam Rifles camps, looted Aizawl, Lunglei Chawngte and other places. The Government of India sent columns of troops while jet fighters bombed Aizawl, the first time the Central Government had ever used air power against its own people to quell a movement. The Indian government declared MNF as an outlawed organization in 1967 and the bush war continued. A Mizo District Council delegation met then Prime Minister Indira Gandhi in May 1971 and demanded statehood for Mizos separating from Assam. The Centre converted the Mizo hills into a Union Territory (U.T) in July 1971 with an assurance that it would be elevated to the status of state later. A MNF delegation led by Laldenga met Prime Rajiv Gandhi on February 15, 1985. The MNF used the opportunity to come overground; Statehood was pledged and a peace accord was signed on June 30, 1986. The state of Mizoram was formed on February 20, 1987.

In May 2007, a new armed group, the Singlung Tiger Force was formed, which later became the Singlung People's Liberation Army (SPLA). It is an armed group whose cadres are drawn from the Hmar community having its bases in the border areas of Manipur-Mizoram-Myanmar. The ideology behind the formation of the outfit was to defend the rights of the indigenous Singlung people affected by the proposed construction of Tuirial and Tipaimukh multi-purpose hydel project in their area including the adjoining border areas of Manipur and Mizoram. However, on 17 July 2009, 64 cadres of SPLA laid down their arms and surrendered to the Mizoram Government.

The displaced Reangs

As mentioned earlier, some 37,000 people violently displaced in ethnic clashes in Mizoram have lived in miserable conditions in six makeshift camps in neighbouring Tripura for over a decade. The Reangs also called Brus live in Mizoram, Tripura and Assam. In Mizoram they are settled in the valleys along the banks of Longai and Teirei rivers in Aizawl and Mamit district and the Karnafuli River in Lunglei and Chhimtuipui districts. These areas are predominantly hilly and surrounded by deep forests.

The Reangs took shelter in evacuee camps in Tripura's Kanchanpur sub-division of North Tripura district since 1997 following ethnic conflicts with the Mizos. The exodus began following the violence against them after the Bru National Union (BNU) (a political organization of the Reangs /Brus formed in the 1990s) passed a resolution in September 1997 demanding an Autonomous District Council in Mizoram under the Sixth Schedule. This demand sparked off a controversy. The Mizo Zillai Pall (MZP), the powerful Mizo student organization sharply reacted: "If the Reangs wanted to divide or disintegrate Mizoram further, it would be better that they go away. The resolution demanding Autonomous District Council (ADC) could not be accepted by MZP. If the Reangs go ahead with their plan, the MZP was ready to fight against such a demand. Mizoram is the only land Mizos have and it could not be lost to foreigners or other communities." [5]

The Reangs were attacked by Mizo groups, alleged with police

---

[5]   , 20 Dec 1997

connivance, houses were torched, hundreds were killed, belongings and livestock were looted. There were allegations of rape. When the victims lodged complaints, police officials advised them to vacate their houses otherwise their homes could be attacked again. Those inmates who fled to Tripura told a group of visiting journalists that at least 44 villages in Aizawl and Mammit districts were attacked, forcing them to leave their ancestral homes.[6]

The conditions in the evacuee camps remain pathetic. Inmates suffer from malnutrition and diseases like malaria and gastroenteritis and these two illness claim about two hundred people a year. There are acute drinking water problems as most of the tube wells do not function properly. Before the monsoon, all natural sources of potable water like streams and wells at the foot of the hills dry up. Children are forced to climb down 2-3 km to dig pits in the stream beds to collect water. They then trek up the steep hills with their water containers. It is not an easy task.

Official ration allotment for one adult inmate is 600 grams of rice and Rs.5 per day, minors get half this amount. Clothes are distributed to every one once a year. They collect wild potatoes, different type of fruits and edible stems from local forests to supplement this meager diet. Sanitation in the camps is poor. There are no bathrooms or toilets. Inmates bathe in cherras (rivulets), and use open forest as toilet.

Although there has been a baby boom in the camps, the new born face an uncertain future. There are no schools in the camps. The state government had engaged 72 teachers from among the camp residents at the rate of Rs.1,000 per month, under the Sarva Shiksha Abhiyan. But, since there is no school building, the teachers cannot function.

The President of the Mizo Bru Displaced Peoples Forum (MBDPF), Elvis Chorkhy, says, however, that everyone at the camps, except newborn babies, belong to Mizoram and that all have official proof in the form of

---

[6]   , July 2009

[7] Jayanta Bhattacharya, "Mizoram's unwanted citizens"   July 2009 available online at http://infochangeindia.org/index2.php? option=com_content&do_pdf=1&id=7858

citizenship certificates, bank passbooks, ration cards and birth certificates. [7] Tripura Chief Minister Manik Sarkar has also stated that the refugees are from Mizoram and that the Mizo government should take them all back.

The Mizoram chief minister says repatriation will begin only after the identity issue is settled. NGOs are to be engaged to help in the identification process. It has been decided that Rs 30,000 per family will be provided as housing assistance, Rs 50,000 in cash grants, and one year's ration after repatriation. Also special development projects will be launched in Mamit, Kolashib, Lunglei and Aizawl districts in Mizoram.

Chorkhy argues that if the Lais, Maras and Chakmas living in Mizoram have the benefits of tribal district councils, why not the Brus be recognised in the same manner? The repatriation of displaced people hangs in the balance as successive governments have given no clear assurances of taking them back and resettling them properly. Former Chief Minister Zoramthanga said on several occasions that only 16,000 of the refugees were from Mizoram and only this figure would be rehabilitated if they are willing to return.

In 2009, Mizoram government has apparently agreed to take back Bru/ Reang refugees sheltered in the camps. The decision was taken at a meeting in Aizawl, on April 31, 2009, between representatives of the Mizoram government, headed by Chief Minister Lalthanhawla, and members of the Mizo Bru Displaced Peoples Forum (MBDPF). Chorkhy claims that the names of a number of Reangs were struck off the voter lists before the assembly elections of May 2009 to prove that the Reangs were not original inhabitants of Mizoram. According to him, the two extremist groups — the Bru National Liberation Front (BNLF) and the Bru Liberation Front of Mizoram (BLFM) have even come 'overground', following the signing of an agreement with the government five years ago. But even they have not been rehabilitated properly.[8]

The refugees' repatriation from Tripura to Mizoram has been stalled by a series of incidents, it was supposed to be started in November 2009 but

---

[8] Ibid.

stopped when a mob in western Mizoram burnt down around 700 tribal houses after an 18-year-old Mizo youth was shot dead by unidentified assailants. Following the arson and violence, about 5,500 displaced Reang tribals took shelter afresh in adjacent north Tripura. However, this entire group returned to Mizoram in May 2010 following official assurances. During a visit that month, Union Home Minister P. Chidambaram had asked the Mizoram government and tribal leaders to help repatriate all 37,000 Reang tribal refugees to their ancestral villages. But till the middle of 2010, the whole process has been stymied by the Mizoram government despite four meetings at senior level in New Delhi since 1997 to break the logjam. The Centre also has not pushed Mizoram too strongly on this although in the past months it has increased its pressure, having dilly-dallied for nearly 13 years. At a meeting on September 23, 2009 attended by then Union Home Secretary, G. K. Pillai, Secretary, Binoy Kumar, Joint Secretary, Nabin Verma, and the Chief Secretaries of the concerned states, it was decided that the camp inmates would be taken back and rehabilitated properly and the entire process would be completed by February 2010.

However, the entire process received a jolt when the November attack on the Reang inhabited areas took place, although this has been resolved. But the larger issue of the peripheral minorities remains unsolved as the 37,000 languish in relief camps in abysmal conditions in Tripura[9].

The impact of this conflict in Mizoram is to be seen on a small neighbouring state, far from Delhi, although that state (Tripura) has virtually resolved its own insurgency-related issues.

---

[9] By January, 2010, the Reangs had returned to Mizoram after a final agreement brokered by the Asia Human Rights Committee of New Delhi

APPENDIX

THE INSURGENT NORTHEAST

E N Rammohan

Assam

Assam has three races of people who migrated into its verdant Brahmaputra valley. The first were the Mongoloid peoples who migrated from the headwaters of the Hwang Ho and the Yangtze Kiang. One group went west from Burma and settled in the Brahmaputra valley and the hills to its north and south. The tribes who diversified in the valley were the Boro Cacharis, Sonowal Cacharis, Dimasa Cacharis, Thengal Cacharis, Karbis, Lalungs or Tiwas, Chutiyas, Morans, Borahi, and Rabhas. Later the Austric, Aryans, and Dravidians came from the Gangetic valley. The Hindus and the Tribals did not seem to have had serious differences and the migratory groups settled down. In the 12th century, the Ahoms a group related to the Shans of Burma migrated to Upper Assam and established their kingdom there. They ruled for 600 years till they were defeated by the Burmese king who also laid waste their beautiful country. The British East India Company came to the rescue and defeated the Burmese in 1826. When the British occupied Upper Assam, they found that the land was very sparsely populated. They also found that tea grew well there. By the end of the century, the British had spread tea gardens all over the foothills to the north and the south of the Brahmaputra valley.

They found that the indigenous population was not willing to work in the tea gardens, so they imported Adivasi tribals from Southeastern and Central India. Then they found that the indigenous population was not capable of growing surplus rice to feed the tea garden labour. In neighbouring East Bengal, the Bengali Muslim population was already running short of cultivable land. The British consciously encouraged immigration of Bengali Muslims from East Bengal districts. They came in hordes and settled in Goalpara, Kamrup, and Nowgong districts. By 1931, just thirty years after the migration had started, more than ten million Bengali Muslim peasants had settled in the above three districts. C.S.Mullen the Census Commissioner of Assam recorded this. Later the government of Sir Saadullah again encouraged the Bengali Muslims to settle by de-reserving grazing reserves for them. There was a growing disillusionment among Assam's intellectuals and some voiced sentiments that Assam should be a separate country like Burma. The third group of people who played a significant role in alienating the people of Assam was the Marwaris whom the British brought, to be their middlemen as Assam at that time had a barter economy. Within a short time of their arrival, the Marwaris had opened shops in all tea gardens, diversified into the grain trade and by the time of independence had established a complete grip on the trade and commerce of Assam. The last group that the British brought was the Bengali Hindus from East and West Bengal. They were brought to work as clerks in the tea gardens and the oil and coal industries that had developed in Upper Assam.Thus by the time of independence, the Bengali Muslim peasant was grabbing the land of the caste Hindu and the tribals, the Bengali babu had an upper hand over the Assamese babu in the job market, the Marwari had taken firm control of the grain and essential supplies, textiles and every other item of commerce. The alienation of the Assamese was already complete.

In the run up to independence, Assam was almost lost to Pakistan. The Congress leadership in Delhi did not object to Assam being included with Bengal in the boundary commission. It was Mahatma Gandhi who interceded on behalf of the Assam leaders and reversed this decision. Later after independence, the Assam Congress leaders were rebuffed by Nehru when they objected to more than three lakh Bengali Hindu refugees being sent to Assam. In 1957, the centre decided to construct a 3.3 million-ton refinery at Barauni by taking the crude from the oil fields in Assam by a 700-kilometre pipeline. There was a huge agitation, the first of its kind in India after independence. Ultimately a 0.65-ton mini refinery was conceded to Assam at Noonmati. This only confirmed the feeling that Assam was getting step brotherly treatment from Delhi.

In the sixties the Marwaris who controlled the grain trade created huge shortages in rice by smuggling out large quantities to East Pakistan. Hojai the rice bowl of Assam was not giving one kilogram of paddy to the state levy for years together. This boiled up into a an anti national agitation on 26 January 1968 when the national flag was desecrated at Guwahati after the flag hoisting and mobs of students calling themselves the *Lachit sena* burnt Fancy Bazaar, the business centre of Guwahati and crores worth of property went up in smoke. Interestingly not a single person was injured. Once again the Centre planned to construct a refinery outside Assam. The students organised a huge agitation. The war cry in the agitation was- "*Tez deem Tel ni diun*" (We will give blood not oil). The centre relented and established the refinery at Bongaigaon. The conclusion was that the centre was trying to treat Assam like a colony.

Two issues had by now crystallized in Assam- the continually deteriorating economic situation and the continuing illegal migration from East Pakistan. The tea, oil and coal industries in Assam did not seem to improve the economy of the state. Most of the sales tax on tea was being paid to West Bengal as most of the HQs of the tea companies were at Calcutta. The royalty paid to Assam for its oil was a paltry Rs. 42 per tonne. The centre refused to raise the royalty. Most of the jobs in the Central Government departments and in the public sector in Assam were going to Bengalis and outsiders. The feeling began to take ground among Assamese people that the centre was continuing to treat Assam like a colony.

Throughout the fifties and the sixties, Bengali Muslim and Hindu immigration continued unabated mainly abetted by a venal bureaucracy. However a sizeable number of immigrant Muslim and Hindu Bengalis were detected and deported. In the early seventies, the concept of committed bureaucracy that had been fostered by the party in power at Delhi brought about a sea change in the administration. The politicians of Assam and the Centre realized that the immigrant Bengali Muslim was an infallible vote bank and the bureaucracy when made to bend would willingly crawl. After this, detection and deportation of immigrant Bengali Muslims simply stopped in Assam. At this time the sitting member of the Lok Sabha in Mangaldoi constituency died in office and a by-election was called. A large number of representations were sent to the Chief Election Commissioner (CEC) at Delhi that there were a number of foreigners in the electoral rolls of Mangaldoi constituency. The CEC had the matter enquired and made a press statement that the electoral rolls of Mangaldoi had to be revised before going for the by- poll. Just at that time the Janata Dal Government was toppled and a lame duck Prime Minister Charan Singh was installed with the Congress driving from behind. The Muslim lobby immediately petitioned the Congress that the polling in Mangaldoi should be conducted without revising the electoral rolls. The CEC humbly recanted and announced that the by-poll would be conducted in Mangaldoi on the basis of the 1976 electoral roll. By that time hundreds of petitions had been filed about foreigners in the electoral rolls of Mangaldoi. The reaction in Assam was electric and the All Assam Students Union (AASU) and the Assam Jatiyatibadi Yuba Chatra Parishad formed the Assam Gana Sangram Parishad and started the Foreigners movement on 6 November 1979 with mass Satyagraha. The movement snowballed with thousands of people courting arrest. Not since the 1942 civil disobedience movement had India seen such an agitation. The State administration came to a halt.

The Centre tried their best to woo the leaders of the movement. The issue was the question of the cut off year for detection of foreigners. The year was 1951 as per the Citizenship act. In 1971 after the liberation of Bangladesh, during the Indira-Mujib talks, Mujibur Rehman had told our Prime Minister that he would not take back any citizens of East Pakistan who had migrated to India before 25 March 1971, the date of formation of the Government of Bangladesh in exile in India. Our Prime Minister agreed to this. After this the Government of India was maintaining that the cut off year was 25 March 1971 an illegal premise, as there was no legal basis for this. The people of Assam had a very strong case and the Government of

India had no case at all. Despite their best efforts, the Assam Gana Sangram Parishad would not budge. The Foreigners Movement soon developed an extremist wing. After four years, The Government of India forced an election on the state in February 1983.

The people of Assam boycotted the election. The state went on a natural curfew from 2 February 1983 till 21 February 1983. In this span of 21 days, more than three thousand people died in ethnic clashes and in police firings. The elections were a farce, with hardly 20 polling booths being opened in most of the Assamese constituencies. In fact in more than a dozen Assamese constituencies the polling had to be countermanded. In several polling booths, the polling figures were 350 or 400 against an electoral roll of one lakh. The elections were patently illegal. Police had to open fire on mobs several hundreds strong opposing the election in dozens of places. Assam was divided on ethnic lines. The Centre allowed a Congress government to be formed on the basis of this illegal election. It was this terrible election that set the youth of Assam to take the insurgent path to fight against the injustice meted out to them by the centre. A group of young men from the villages of Jheraigaon and Lakwa in upper Assam had met at the Ranghar in Nazira in 1979 to discuss the problems of illegal migration in Assam. Now they decided that they had no alternative but to take to the gun. They went to Dimapur and met the leaders of the NSCN there, who warmly welcomed them. By the end of the year the first cadres of the United Liberation Front of Assam were being sent to the NSCN camp in Burma for training. To add insult to injury, the Home Ministry legislated an act- the Illegal Migrants Determination by Tribunal act (IMDT) in 1983 after the terrible elections. The foreigners act was kept in abeyance and the IMDT was substituted for it in Assam. This was absurd. How could there be two acts for the same offence? Under Foreigners act the onus was on the accused to prove that he was an Indian citizen, while under the IMDT act it was for the prosecution to prove that he was an Indian citizen. The act was illegal and unconstitutional.

The Congress government was in position till they were asked to step down by the Centre in 1985. Till then the ULFA was not seen in action.

During the elections of 1985, there was no sign of the ULFA cadres influencing the election campaign or the polls later. It is only after the Assam Gana Parishad (AGP) formed the government that the ULFA started their insurgent activities. This was the first mistake of the insurgent group and of course of the AGP government. With the tacit backing of the state government, the ULFA did not have the police behind their backs. They were thus not blooded like all insurgent groups. They did not have to attack police stations, or armed police camps to snatch weapons. They only robbed two banks in their march forward. Later they found that extortion was a much easier way to collect funds for purchasing arms and rations for their cadres. The AGP government neutered the police. ULFA made their main base camp in Lakhipathar Reserve Forest near Digboi police station. No directions were given to the police to encircle and attack the base camp of the ULFA. By this time the ULFA leaders had linked up with the Kachin Independent Army (KIA) in northern Burma and their cadres were being trained there. Very soon the ULFA coffers were bulging. This led to the second big mistake of this insurgent group. Like in many insurgencies, besides highly committed rural youth, lumpen elements from the urban areas also joined the ULFA. Many lumpen elements became second level leaders. Large sums of money extorted were not deposited in the central treasury of the organisation. This cancer of corruption was to be the nemesis of this insurgent group. There was a pall of fear over Assam from 1985 to 1990, when the Centre declared Presidents rule and deployed the army in Assam. The Army operations were one sided. There was hardly a single ambush on the army. The ULFA had not been blooded like the Naga underground army or the Mizo National Front (MNF). But they had the support of the people. This helped them to elude capture and for almost nine months, not a single first line leader was captured.

The AGP government had a very fine chance of taking the state forward when they formed the government in 1985. They were fresh, new to politics and government and they had the chance of a lifetime to take Assam away from the festering corruption of the previous Congress government. Regrettably they threw away this chance to make history and became as corrupt as their predecessor government.

The counterinsurgency operations were proceeding well under Presidents rule. When the elections were called prematurely after just five months of Presidents rule, the whole picture changed. The Chief Minister directed that all surrenders should be made before him. He allowed every single important ULFA leader who surrendered before him to keep his weapon. He organised them into a mafia that continued to extort money from the business community, this time with the police being made to look the other way. The people of Assam was now at their wits end, with the ULFA extorting money from the people, and the SULFA as the surrendered ULFA were called also extorting money from the people with the police looking the other way.

By now the ULFA had been denied sanctuary by the KIA and they perforce had to go to Bangladesh for help. The ULFA cadres were welcomed by the Bangladesh Directorate General Forces Intelligence (DGFI) and the Pakistan ISI in Dacca. Very soon ULFA cadres were going to Peshawar for training and the ISI had arranged to bring arms for them and the NSCN (IM) from Thailand. The ULFA had to pay a price for this. One of the main causes for the insurgency was the illegal immigration of Bengalis from Bangladesh to Assam that was being colluded by the Congress government. Now the ULFA was taking sanctuary in the same Bangladesh. The organisation lost a good deal of support from the people of Assam on this issue. This reached a turning point during the Kargil war when ULFA asked the people of Assam to support Pakistan in this war. The call came when an emotional funeral was being given to Captain Jintu Gogoi a young Assamese army officer who was killed in Kargil. ULFA lost a great measure of support on this issue too. Later a number of children were killed in Dhemaji by a bomb detonated by ULFA cadres. Today the ULFA has very little support from the people of Assam.

In 1990, a group of young Bodo men set up an insurgent group called the Bodo Security Force (BdSF) in Udalguri sub division of Assam. The leader was a young Bodo postgraduate student of the North Eastern Hill University, Shillong. He had earlier studied in the Union Christian College Barapani, a Baptist college. Several Naga leaders of the NSCN had also studied in this college. The majority of the cadres of the BdSF were Christians. Their demand was for a separate country for the Bodo people of Assam. In 1991, the ULFA had a meeting with the BdSF leaders across the border in Bhutan where the BdSF had set up three camps and it was decided that the ULFA would also set up camps there. Within a couple of years, the ULFA had shifted its Council and General HQs to Bhutan. The ULFA leaders took the BdSF leaders to Bangladesh and both groups brought the arms they had purchased through the ISI to their camps in Bhutan. The BdSF changed its name to the National Democratic Front for Bodoland (NDFB). Unlike the ULFA, the NDFB was a very disciplined organisation and its cadres were very honest and all money extorted from tea gardens and businessmen were deposited in their GHQ. Both the ULFA and the NDFB kept good relations with the Bhutan Government officials by investing money with their business ventures. With continual pressure from the Government of India, the Bhutan government finally directed the ULFA and the NDFB to leave their country. When they did not listen, the Bhutan army attacked their camps and both the ULFA and the NDFB lost all their weapons in their camps. Several cadres of both groups were arrested. The ULFA regrouped in Burma with Kaphlang, but the NDFB was badly hit. Shortly after, they sued for peace and talks started between the Government of India and the NDFB.

Two other small insurgent groups that came up in Assam were the Dima Halam Daoga (DHD) in the North Cachar Hills and the United Peoples Democratic Solidarity (UPDS) in Karbi Anglong. Both these insurgent groups came up at the instigation of the NSCN (IM). In North Cachar Hills the District Council was a thoroughly corrupt body and eight families swiped all the development money since inception. The district was still much undeveloped after forty years and the Dimasas took to the gun. The story in Karbi Anglong district was also similar. Both groups are now talking to the government and cease-fire is on.

The insurgencies of Assam are very easy to solve. Ever since independence, the trade in essential supplies is in the hands of the Marwaris in the state. They divert 90 per cent of all food grains brought into the North East into the black market from the railhead itself. The first step is to deploy CRPF at the railheads and see that all civil supplies are taken to the depots from the railheads. From there they should be carried to the wholesalers and retailers under CRPF escorts. Clean officers should be posted in the Food Corporation of India and in the state supply departments.

Both the AGP and the Congress governments have been very corrupt. Both these governments swindled all development money sent to the state from 1991 till 2001. Today the state is on the verge of financial bankruptcy. Assam has had no green revolution. It has only one or two small weirs worth the name. Irrigation projects should be set up in all the districts immediately so the people can do double cropping. After this, development projects should be set up and monitored by concurrent audits at every stage before funds are released. The nexus between the politicians, bureaucrats and contractors should be broken by posting clean and honest officers in crucial, cutting edge levels. If this is carefully monitored the insurgent groups of Assam will whither away. The border with Bangladesh must be strongly fenced and fitted with an electronic screen so that infiltration is completely controlled. If this can be done on the western border, why not on the eastern wing?

In late 2005 the Supreme Court repealed the IMDT act as unconstitutional and illegal. The Government, however, to preserve its vote bank has brought the provisions of the IMDT act by amending the Foreigners Tribunal order under the rules of the Foreigners act. This is a certain recipe to revive the ULFA.

Tripura

The insurgency in Tripura is due to one cause only, the domination of the tribal state by Bengali Hindus and Muslims after partition in 1947 and the second class treatment given to the tribal people by the caste Hindu Bengalis.

Tripura was a kingdom ruled by a king of the Tripuri tribe that migrated into this hill state long before recorded history. The tribes of Tripura all migrated westwards from the headwaters of the Yangtse Kiang and the Hwang Ho along with other Tibeto Burman tribes like the Boro Cacharis of Assam and the Garos of Meghalaya. The tribes that migrated into the Tripura tracts were the Tripuri, Riang or Bru, Jamatia, Halam and Noatia. The Tripuri dominated the other tribes and ruled as the dominant Kingdom of Tripura till it was merged with the Indian Union in 1949.

Migration of Bengali Hindus and probably Muslims into Tripura started from the 14th century. The Tripuri kings encouraged migration and settlement of Bengali Hindus into Tripura to encourage their tribal people to take to wet cultivation. The Tripuri kings also encouraged the Bengali language to the exclusion of Kok Barok, and the other tribal dialects. The tribal percentage was reduced to 50% by 1941. In 1951, just three years after partition, the tribals were reduced to 36.85%. One other interesting factor is also the increasing percentage of conversion of the tribals into Christianity. The figure in 1947 was just 6151. It was 46,472 in 1991.

When a flood of refugees swamped Tripura in 1947, the Congress party was seen to side with the Bengali Hindus. The Communist party of India (CPI) and later the Communist Party Marxist (CPM) sided with the tribals. The tribals formed the *Gana Mukti Parishad* (GMP) in 1948 to protect the civil rights and economic development of the tribals. The GMP organised a rally against smuggling of rice into East Pakistan. The resultant police suppression led to the creation of a guerilla wing in the GMP called the *Shanti Sena*. Khowai sub division became a liberated area. The CPI joined the tribals in their struggle. The GMP became the tribal wing of the party after this.

In 1943, the tribal king had reserved an area of 1950 square miles for tribals and prohibiting transfer of land of tribals to non-tribals. The tidal wave of refugees was so much that the Regent queen dereserved 330 square miles. Worse still, even the reduced area could not be reserved for the tribals. Encroachment and illegal transfer of tribal lands continued. The Tripura land revenue and land reforms act was passed in 1960. This prohibited transfer of tribal land to non-tribals. The provision for restoration of alienated land was however passed only in January 1969 thus regularising land alienated even after the land reform act was passed for nine years. The Bengali lobby was still strong and the Congress party got firmly identified as anti tribal and pro Bengali.

In 1967 tribal leaders set up the Tripura Upa Jati Samity (TUJS). Paradoxically this group strengthened ties with the Congress. In 1979, the Foreigners agitation started in Assam and spread to Tripura. The Left Front supported the tribals. At this moment the Anand Marg stepped in and a number of attacks on CPM meetings took place. Tripura was polarised into two ethnic camps. In the clashes that ensued the police sided with the Bengali Hindus. The tribals killed 380 Bengali Hindus at Mandai. After this the CPM Government asked the Centre for an Autonomous District Council, which the Centre refused. The CPM then opened the Tripura Tribal Areas Autonomous District Council (TTAADC) under the seventh schedule. Meanwhile the TUJS under Bijoy Kumar Hrangkhawl had organised an armed wing and formed the Tripura National Volunteers (TNV). He went to the MNF across the Jampui ridge and linked up with them. He organised a guerilla war against the government from safe bases in the Chittagong Hill Tracts (CHT). He fought a desultory bush war with the government for about ten years. The TUJS had Congress links and this finally brought Hrankhawl overground in 1988. This deal which the Centre signed with Hrankhawl was a mistake because the problems of the tribals had not yet been solved. Several disgruntled leaders of the TNV reneged and formed two insurgent groups the National Liberation Front of Tripura (NLFT) led by Dhananjoy Reang and the All Tripura Tiger Force (ATTF) led by Lalit Debbarma and Ranjit Debbarma. The NLFT patronised by the Congress and the ATTF by the CPM, established bases in the hill ranges north of Tripura in Bangladesh and in the CHT in the south. Both groups extorted money from the *mahajans* in the towns in the valleys and also from the tea gardens. The decade from 1990 saw a proliferation in the activities of these two groups. The NLFT linked up with the NSCN (IM) and were trained by them. The ATTF did not link up with the NSCN (IM) but got sanctuary in Bangladesh helped by the DGFI who also helped them to procure weapons. The 1990s saw a spate of kidnapping for ransom and killing of innocent Bengali Hindus by gangs of the ATTF attacking the civilian supporters of the Congress and the NLFT attacking the supporters of the CPM.

By 2002, the Tripura Police was able to break the kidnapping/ ransom nexus of both the main groups. The NLFT split into several factions and two of them surrendered by 2005. The ATTF severed its links with the CPM and is holding out in the CHT. It has linked up with the UNLF of Manipur and the ULFA of Assam.

Tripura has the cleanest of all governments in India. Corruption is not a cause of the insurgency. The TTAADC has however not been able to carry out sustainable development in the tribal areas. The interior areas still do not have roads connecting all the villages to the towns. Block Development officers are not able to freely visit interior tribal areas and supervise development projects because of lack of security. They disburse grants in cash. This is frittered away by the tribals in the interiors. The BSF are thinly deployed on the borders and have not been able to prevent the gangs of the NLFT and the ATTF from infiltrating ambushing a convoy and returning to their bases in the CHT or in the north into Bangladesh.

The formula for finishing the insurgency in Tripura is as follows:-

1. Divide the tribal areas into small development blocks.

2. Deploy sufficient force in a few adjacent selected blocks along the border.

3. Deploy a battalion of BSF in border outposts two kilometres apart along this stretch. Fence the border and also complete a border road behind the fence. This should seal the villages behind from access from across the border.

4. Construct roads linking the villages to the nearest town under complete security.

5. Construct a water supply scheme in each of the villages in this block.

6. Formulate a development plan for all the villages in this block pertaining to the possible schemes that would suit the village be it horticulture, agriculture, piggery, poultry, forestry, pisciculture growing orchids etc. In each project the local people of the village must be involved and only the expert should be brought from outside.

7.   In each project security force should be deployed till the project comes to maturity and the produce escorted to the market in the towns. Each family should thus become self-sustaining.

8.   The whole border should meanwhile be fenced and the border road completed.

9.   Other blocks can then be taken up and the experiment repeated.

10. It will be seen that the quantum of security forces required is very high. Its optimum level should be maintained so that the insurgent groups cannot penetrate and extort money or ambush and attack the civilians of the block concerned.

In general all land alienated from the tribals should be returned to them. Tribals should administer the TTAADC areas as far as possible. They have been alienated. They should gradually be encouraged to lead the state in all fields.

Manipur

The causes of the insurgency in Manipur are easily identifiable. There is a strong sense of alienation among the Meitei people. There is today a sizeable group of intellectuals among them who advocate separation from India. The Governments mistakes are also easily identifiable. The Central government has from the time Manipur was made an Union Territory treated the state like a colony of India. The bureaucrats who went from Delhi in collusion with the Marwaris and other traders from India's mainland thoroughly corrupted the administration. Firstly they saw to it that all civil supplies coming from the mainland was diverted at the railheads itself. The people of Manipur have not known a white economy since its absorption into India. In this process the local businessmen, bureaucrats and politicians also joined the bandwagon. Development money was swindled in crores. Since there was no real development, there was no generation of employment in industries, horticulture, and a hundred other ventures. There was only the Government for milking and it was bled dry by the unholy trio of the politician, the bureaucrat and the trader. When the unemployed frustrated angry youngmen took to the gun, they added to the unholy trio in taking the largest share of the money diverted from development. Extortion has become pervasive in Manipur, particularly in the valley. All government servants contribute to different insurgent groups. The cashier or accountant of each department deducts the contribution and pays to the insurgent group. When the government offices are cordoned by the CRPF, the insurgents visit the heads of departments at their houses. The politicians pay the highest shares to the insurgent groups as they get the biggest cut of the development money.

The two biggest groups of the Meitei insurgents were the PLA and the PREPAK. They were at their peak in the late 1970s looting banks, attacking police stations and ambushing security patrols to get their weapons. The Army deployed in the valley, was able to break the back of these two groups after sustained operations capturing the chief of the PLA and killing many of their top leaders. Unfortunately the causes of the insurgency were not addressed and both the groups revived in the 1990s. The UNLF that was raised in 1964 as a social organisation now joined the PLA and the PREPAK. Two other groups that sprung up were the KCP and the KYKL. All these groups took advantage of two factors in Manipur that gave a distinct advantage to guerilla warfare. These were the lack of roads and a vast hinterland. Both these factors were in Chandel and Churachandpur districts. Both districts had a long unpoliced border with Burma. The border to a depth of 100 kilometres was thickly forested and without any roads. All the groups took full advantage of these two factors and established base camps deep inside this hinterland. Across the border in Burma from Chandel district was the Kebaw valley and the Somra tracts, while across the border from Churachandpur district was the Chin Hills. The Burmese government had very little presence in the Chin Hills and in the Somra tracts. Also, China after its economic liberalisation had set up an industrial base in the Kunming and Yunnan area. There were several arms factories set up in this industrial complex. Some of the insurgent groups in northern Burma that had surrendered to the Burmese army had been rehabilitated in drug cartels and as clandestine weapon dealers. The PLA, UNLF, PREPAK, KYKL and the KCP were able to purchase arms from these arms dealers. The UNLF has besides AK rifles, LMGs, rocket launchers and even some air defence guns. The PLA and the KYKL both had links with the NSCN (IM) and procured weapons from them through the ISI and the DGFI links from Bangladesh. The whole tract of several thousand hectares comprising Churachandpur and part of Tamenglong districts bounded by the Thangjing hills in the east, national highway 53 in the north, the Man Bahadur road in the west and the Burmese border in the south is a liberated area. In 2000, the BSF was given the task of clearing four subdivisions in this rectangle of land that was occupied by the PLA and the UNLF for three years. These were the subdivisions of Thinghat, Henglep, Thanglon and Parbung. All the four subdivisions were cleared and the Indian flag flew over these four subdivisions again. Regrettably, the state government did not cooperate and send the civil administration to reestablish their authority. In 2001 the BSF was withdrawn and the insurgents returned. In 2005, the Army was deployed extensively in both Chandel and Churachandpur districts. They have reoccupied the four subdivisions and also cleared the area of south Chandel. The civil administration is yet to reestablish their presence in these areas.

Besides the Meitei groups, a Kuki group called the Kuki National Army (KNA) was set up in 1992 to fight against the NSCN (IM). The KNA has split up into at least five to six factions during the last fifteen years. Each group is a rag-tag band that supports a politician during elections and gains patronage from him for shares from the development funds. All these groups should be disarmed. Some of them are being used to fight against the Meitei groups- the UNLF and the PLA. This should be forthwith discontinued and all these rag-tag groups asked to disband. The cadres of these groups can be rehabilitated by absorbing them in the Paramilitary forces.

What is the answer for Manipur? The government has today a fine chance of retrieving the situation. It has to prepare a detailed plan to develop the hinterland in Manipur. With the Army in position, roads should be constructed connecting all villages to the nearest towns. The Border Roads should do this work. Each village should get a water supply system. Once this is done, experts from different fields, poultry, fisheries, horticulture, piggery, dairy farming, forestry, cultivation of orchids and medicinal plants should prepare detailed plans for the two districts. In each project the local people should be involved in the execution. Only the expert should be from outside. It should be possible to transform the two districts in a time frame of two to three years, after which the same plan should be implemented in Ukhrul, Senapati and Tamenglong districts. Development grants should be released in installments for each project, ensuring that concurrent audits are done at each stage before releasing the next installment. The audit parties should be detailed from states outside the northeast.

All convoys of civil supplies should be escorted by the CRPF from the road heads to the depots in Imphal and from there to the district HQs and thence to every single village. This will break the nexus between the trader, the bureaucrat, the politician and the insurgent in the state. This one measure will turn the people of the state against the insurgents.

As this plan is being executed, the valley must be divided into sectors and strongly policed by the Army or Paramilitary forces to prevent the insurgent groups from reorganising there. Secondly a border road should be constructed along the Indo-Burma border in Arunachal Pradesh, Nagaland, Manipur and Mizoram and a string of border outposts constructed and manned by the Border Security Force.

Nagaland

The initial cause for the insurgency in the Naga Hills was the alienation that a section of their leaders felt that they were not like the plains Hindu or Muslim peoples. This sense of alienation was fostered by the proselytisation carried out by the British from the eighteenth century. This was compounded by the policy of the Central Government to flood the state, when it was created, with development funds followed up by sending a band of contractors that acquired the dubious name of the Delhi durbar who corrupted the politicians and bureaucrats of the state and brought back ninety per cent of the development funds sent to the state to Delhi by carrying out development work and supplying stores on paper. Unhappily, the bureaucracy in conjunction with the politicians and the Marwaris who controlled all essential commodities like rice, sugar, petrol, kerosene and later gas ensured from the beginning that all these supplies were diverted to the black-market from the railheads itself. As a result the states of Nagaland, Manipur, Mizoram, and Arunachal Pradesh have only known a black economy from inception.

The mistakes made by the Government of India when the Naga insurgency broke out exacerbated the situation in the Naga and Manipur hills in the late fifties and sixties. The Central Government enacted the Assam Disturbed Area Act in 1955 and the Armed Forces Special Powers Act in 1958 and deployed the Army to tackle the situation. The Police and the Judiciary were sidelined in the process and inevitably excesses occurred during operations. The policy measure of the Army to regroup the Naga Villages also deeply alienated the people. This was a leaf picked from the Malayan insurgency. In Malaya the people regrouped were Chinese settlers in the Rubber plantations. They were living in temporary shanties. The Naga villages were ancient with sacred groves. The last major action of the Para Military Assam Rifles was the incident at Oinam village in Senapati district of Manipur. On 9 July 1987, a group of the NSCN (IM) overran the Assam Rifles post at Oinam village killing a Junior Commissioned Officer and eight soldiers capturing 90 Self Loading Rifles, 27 Sten Guns, 10 Light Machine Guns two 2" Mortars and a large quantity of ammunition. In the reaction to the incident, the Army almost flattened Oinam village, killing 14 persons, none of whom were cadres of the NSCN (IM). Oinam has passed into the legend of the Naga struggle for independence and songs are sung during memorial services for the innocent people who were killed there.

In 1997 a cease-fire was signed with the NSCN (IM) leaders and a Cease-Fire Monitoring Group (CFMG) was set up. Unfortunately, the Government of India made two mistakes. At the time of signing the cease-fire agreement, the NSCN (IM) had several camps in the Naga districts of Manipur. The Cease-fire was signed for Nagaland only, but was unofficially extended to Manipur. Secondly the Government of Nagaland did nothing to enforce the conditions prescribed for the insurgent group. The NSCN (IM) had already established a well-oiled extortion network in Nagaland and Manipur. After the cease-fire, the NSCN (IM) continued to extort money from all businessmen and the people with impunity. The cease-fire is now nine years old. During these nine years, the NSCN (IM) has flouted virtually all the conditions of the cease fire with impunity and extorted crores of rupees that have enabled the group to set up offices in Bangkok, Manila, and Amsterdam. They have also brought in considerable number of weapons, purchasing them with the assistance of the ISI and the DGFI and bringing them by coastal steamer to Cox's Bazaar and then taking them overland via the Chittagong Hill Tracts (CHT), Mizoram, Manipur to Nagaland and then to Assam. Today the NSCN (IM) has about 5500 cadres and as many weapons.

The NSCN (IM) has a list of unreasonable demands. They want a separate constitution, with complete autonomy of administration, with permission to retain their armed cadres as their army. They want a separate flag. They of course want the Government of India to finance their revenue and development expenditure. They obviously do not want inconvenient institutions like the Comptroller and Auditor General, the Income Tax Department and the Supreme Court.

The Nagas have no case whatsoever for a greater Nagaland. Their claims on the North Cachar Hills and Karbi Anglong district and Khonsa district of Arunachal Pradesh are not justified by demography. There can be no question of detaching the Naga majority districts of Manipur, as this was a country ruled by its kings for more than 2000 years with a well-defined boundary, before it was merged in to India. There can be simply no question of granting any kind of autonomy to any state in India, be it Kashmir or Nagaland as this would open a Pandora's Box and a hundred different groups in different parts of India would raise similar demands. Government of India can and should immediately create District Councils in all the five hill districts of Manipur and leave development to them in these five districts.

The social bodies in Nagaland like the Naga Ho Ho, the Naga Mothers body and the Baptist Church do not want the cease fire to be abrogated after nine long years. The Government of India has committed several grievous mistakes in the least nine years of the cease-fire. They have not enforced the conditions of the cease-fire. They have allowed the NSCN (IM) to openly extort money from the business community. Frankly the writ of the Government today runs only in the precincts of the Raj Bhavan in Kohima. The first step should be to firmly and gradually stop all extortion by detailing escorts and guards for the private sector. They should then ensure that all civil supplies are made available to the remotest village at the correct price. The people of Nagaland have not known what the white market is since its birth. The Government of India should then talk to the NSCN (K) and to the old NNC along with the NSCN (IM). They should confine all armed cadres of the NSCN (IM) in camps and see that all weapons are surrendered to the Government. They should then be taken back and issued to the Army or the Paramilitary forces. The cadres of the two NSCN groups should then be absorbed in the paramilitary forces of the country. If the NSCN (IM) does not agree, we should be ready to take them on again in a fresh round of jungle war. There is no doubt that we can call their bluff.

CONTRIBUTORS

Dr. Sanjoy Hazarika is a journalist, editor and film maker. An authority on the Northeast India, he has traveled extensively in the region and its neighbouring areas in connection with C-NES projects. He is Chair and Professor, Centre for North East Studies, Jamia Millia Islamia, New Delhi and Consulting Editor, Sunday Guardian. He was consulting Editor at the Statesman and Research Professor at the Centre for Policy Research, New Delhi. He has made a series of documentary films on the region especially on the Brahmaputra River. He is Convener of the CNES- Setu National Media Fellowship involving journalists from the North East and other parts of the country. A former correspondent for the New York Times and author of several books including *Strangers of the Mist*, *Tales of War and Peace from India's North East*. Dr Hazarika was a member of the first National Security Advisory Board (1998-1999) and a member of the advisory panel (North East) for the National Commission to Review the Working of the Constitution. He is a former member of Committee to Review the Armed Forces Special Power Act (AFSPA), and a member of (ICSSR), National Council of the Indian Council of Social Science Research.

Prof N Mohendro Singh is a retired Professor in Economics, Manipur University with more than thirty years of experience in teaching and research. He has published numerous articles and authored four books.

Prof. Samir Kumar Das is a Professor of Political Science at the University of Calcutta, Kolkata and the Research Coordinator of Calcutta Research Group (CRG). He specializes in and writes on issues of ethnicity, security, migration, rights and justice. His publications include *Ethnicity, Nation and*

Security: Essays on Northeastern India (2004), *Regionalism in Power* (1998) and *ULFA – A Political Analysis* (1994).

Dr. Sanjeeb Kakoty is Faculty, Sustainable Development, Rajiv Gandhi Indian Institute of Management, Shillong, Meghalaya. He did his MA in history from NEHU and went on to do his PhD by adopting technology and social formation to understand and explain historical change. Dr. Kakoty has a number of publications to his credit. He has also worked with the Ministry of External Affairs in formulation of the Look East Policy and the Ministry of Commerce for studying the Potential and Problems for trade between North East and South East Asia.

Dr. N. Vijaylakshmi Brara is a Ph.D in Sociology from Jawaharlal Nehru University, New Delhi. Currently, she is a Reader, Centre for Manipur Studies, Manipur University. Dr. Brara's areas of interest are gender dynamics, the cultural studies and the polity. She has been working and researching the Northeast India for the last 18 years. Besides, she also has various papers and articles to her credit. She has also worked with the National Women Commission to bring out a report on the Situational Analysis of Girls and Women in Manipur. She has also been associated with Institute of Social Sciences, New Delhi to work on the local Self-Governments in the North East – especially in the areas of inclusion and exclusion.

Dr Udayon Misra is former Professor of English at Dibrugarh University, Assam. He is currently National Fellow at Indian Council of Social Research, New Delhi. He has written extensively on socio-political issues related to the Northeastern region and his publications include *The Periphery Strikes Back: Challenges to the Nation-State in Assam and Nagaland* (2000); *Transformation of Assamese Identity: A Historical Survey* (2001); *Nation-Building and Development in North-East India* (ed) (1991); and *North-East India: Quest for Identity* (1988).

Mr. Jayanta Bhattacharaya is a journalist and currently working as Bureau Chief of Press Trust of India (PTI) at Agartala, Tripura. He is a media fellow of National Foundation for India and Calcutta Research Group. He has worked with BBC, Sunday Magazine, ABP Publications, Guwahati

112

Bureau Chief of Television Bazaar. He has also worked on a project *Impact of Conflict on Women in Tripura* sponsored by C-NES and National Commission for Women.

Mr. E.N. Rammohan IPS (Retd) is former Director General of Border Security Force. Post retirement, he was Adviser to the Governor of Manipur. Recently, he conducted the one man enquiry to probe the massacre of the CRPF personnel by the Naxalites at Dantewada, Chhattisgarh.

CSA PUBLICATIONS

CONFLICT RESOLUTION AND PEACE BUILDING

1. Conflict Resolution and Peace Building in Sri Lanka

2. Federalism and Conflict Resolution in Sri Lanka

3. Peace Process in Sri Lanka: Challenges & Opportunities

4. Conflict over Fisheries in the Palk Bay Region

5. Conflict in Sri Lanka: The Road Ahead

6. Peace and Conflict Resolution: Emerging Ideas

7. From Winning the War to Winning Peace: Post War Rebuilding of the Society in Sri Lanka

8. Internal Conflicts in Myanmar: Transnational Consequences

9. Internal Conflicts in Nepal: Transnational Consequences

10. The Naxal Threat: Causes, State Responses and Consequences

11. Conflict in Sri Lanka: Internal and External Consequences

SECURITY STUDIES

12. US and the Rising Powers: India and China

13. Maritime Security in the Indian Ocean Region: Critical Issues in Debate

14. Public Perceptions of Security in India: Results of a National Survey

15. Essential Components of National Security

16.   Economic Growth and National Security

17.   Security Dimensions of India and Southeast Asia

18.   India & ASEAN: Non-Traditional Security Threats

19.   Emerging Challenges to Energy Security in the Asia Pacific

20.   Security Dimensions of Peninsular India

21.   Socio-Economic Security of Peninsular India

CIVIL SOCIETY AND GOVERNANCE

22.   Civil Society and Governance in Modern India

23.   Civil Society in Conflict Situations

24.   Civil Society and Human Security: South & Southeast Asian Experiences

www.ingramcontent.com/pod-product-compliance
Lightning Source LLC
Chambersburg PA
CBHW060420100426
42812CB00030B/3256/J